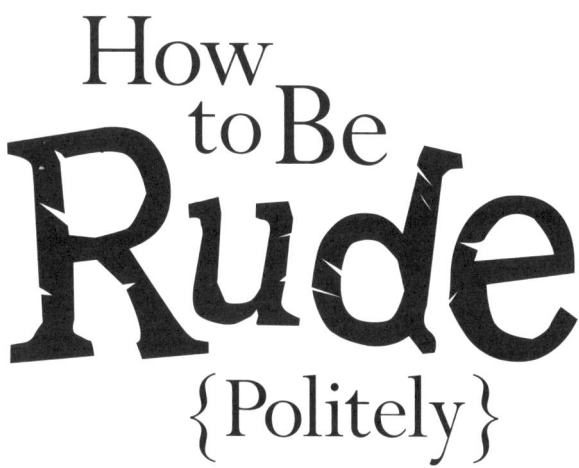

How to Be Rude
{Politely}

by Don Marsh

Illustrations by
Daniel Pearlmutter

Copyright © 2010, Reedy Press, LLC
All rights reserved.

Reedy Press
PO Box 5131
St. Louis, MO 63139

No part of this publication may be reproduced or transmitted in any form or by any means, electronic or mechanical, including photocopy, recording, or any information storage and retrieval system, without permission in writing.

Permissions may be sought directly from the publisher at the above address.

Library of Congress Control Number: 2010924181

ISBN: 978-1-933370-57-6

Printed in the United States of America
10 11 12 13 14   5 4 3 2 1

Contents

Introduction: Not Necessarily Politically Correct Etiquette, Excuses, Advice, and Strategies ix

1. How to Get Two Desserts 3

2. Passing the Bread 11

3. When a Friend or Acquaintance Introduces a Baby 14

4. How to Avoid Accepting an Unexpected Invitation, Even When You Don't Have Time to Think of a Good Excuse 25

5. Inviting People to Parties Knowing They Can't Come 32

6. Excuses for Not Going Someplace You Don't Want to Go 37

7. Leaving a Party 41

8. When Your Dog Violates a Neighbor's Lawn 48

9. How to Insult People in Ways That Make You Feel Good and That Make Them Believe Is a Compliment 53

10. Excuses and Other Strategies for Passing Wind 58

11. Upon Discovering a Close Friend or Relative with "Another" Man or Woman 67

12. How to Avoid a Fight 72

13. When Something's Unsightly in a Partner's Nose   83

14. Passing the Buck (or Blaming Others for Your Mistakes)   88

15. Upon Receiving Incorrect Change   94

16. How to Keep Friends from Using Your Pool   98

17. The Toilet Seat   104

18. Upon Inviting All Your Kindergartner's Friends to a Party, and then Realizing You Left Out the Class Brat   110

19. Forgetting Someone's Name   115

20. Changing Subjects When You Have No Interest in What Someone Is Saying, or Don't Understand What They're Talking About   120

21. How to Get Around Forgetting an Anniversary, Birthday, or Some Other Important Occasion   126

22. When Someone Asks You to Guess His or Her Age   136

23. To People Who Complain About Being Overweight   141

24. On Lying   147

Acknowledgment

My special thanks to illustrator Daniel Pearlmutter. This effort would be a lot less than it is (a frightening prospect) were it not for his illustrations. While he may not have made a silk purse out of a sow's ear, he has at least put lipstick on the sow!

Introduction

Not Necessarily Politically Correct Etiquette, Excuses, Advice, and Strategies

This book is provided as a public service. It is not intended to be a complete compilation of not necessarily politically correct etiquette, excuses, advice, and strategies for dealing with life's challenging moments. There will be sequels, hopefully, and eventually we will cover everything necessary to get what you want while saving face.

What follows are some of the more commonplace situations, and, frankly, some of the situations I have encountered and continue to encounter. The subjects are not alphabetical. They are not listed in any particular order. What may be my most important strategy may be least important to you. So, there was no point in my being anything but subjective.

You will recall, I suspect, that Richard Nixon once said, "I am not a crook." Well, let me declare here and now that I am not a liar. Having said that, I also acknowledge that we all have to bend the truth from time to time. Call it fibbing. Call it fabricating. Call it an overactive imagination. Call it what you will. Whatever it is, it is an art. I have more on the subject inside.

Most of what is included here has been carefully researched. In some cases, the strategies, etiquette, and excuses have failed. I submit that every case in which failure has been joined is the result of poor execution rather than poor strategy.

These things work for my friends. But, as you will soon find out, it takes toughness, nerves of steel, intellect, and an uncompromising desire to succeed. If you possess these qualities and want to keep neighborhood kids out of your pool or have been forced to display enthusiasm over a co-worker's baby, read on.

If neither of these things applies to you, read on. Something in here will.

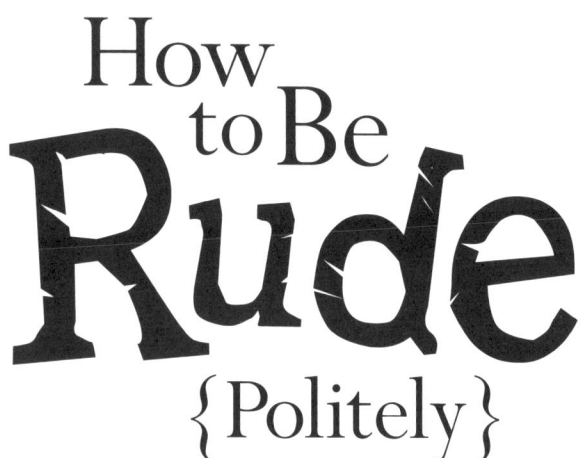

Chapter 1

How to Get Two Desserts

This chapter is dedicated to my wife. She loves desserts and knows no shame in going for seconds. I have seen her single-handedly destroy a simple pan cake at a neighbor's pool party. I have seen her embarrass waiters and waitresses at fine affairs. Once, she browbeat a young lad into giving up his own exotic dessert, a confection so fine, the dinner caterers had only prepared exactly enough for the number of attending guests.

At a company barbecue, or other outdoors events, firing on dessert is no problem. The problem arises when the service is silver and the napkins are linen.

Increasingly, desserts are the pièce de résistance at finer parties. Anyone can whip up a chateaubriand or broil lobster tails. Cordon bleu is a trifle. Roast lamb, kids' play.

Cherries flambé à la Madagascar, or pecan anything, are something quite different. Hosts take increasing pride in putting the finest dessert fare before guests so that their table stands out, stands alone, and sets their soiree well above those sitting above or below the salt. Frequently, it takes much of their resources too. Fine wine or liqueur is often a part of the recipe. And the delicacies are frequently served on crystal or silver or gold, or all three. For this reason, hosts, caterers, and chefs will calculate to the last gram of powdered sugar when planning the number of servings.

Fine desserts do not keep. In my household that is not a problem. Generally, however, hosts paying a caterer do not like to be charged for exotic delicacies that go uneaten. Likewise, the caterer cannot throw it back into a sack like a potato, serve it to domesticated critters, or slice it into indistinguishable parts and make it part of the next appetizer. So, winning seconds is nothing short of an art form.

The first part of the strategy is imperative. You must let people know what you want. You can begin this technique immediately upon sitting down, or shortly after your arrival at the party. A simple, "What's for dessert?" will suffice. Some hosts and hostesses may be taken aback, as might some guests. However, don't worry about it. A hearty laugh when posing the question is a nice defense. An additional, "I have an incorrigible sweet tooth," alerts people to a certain non-threatening free-spirit quality and also lets them know that dessert is important to you.

The trap is sprung at this point, and either the host, hostess, or another guest will often make a point of seeing to it that you get their dessert. And, for your own peace of mind, the answer to your initial question will inform you as to the exact nature of the dessert and determine whether you wish to continue with your strategy. For instance, if it is something with pears or mint jelly, you might wish to abandon the technique immediately. I would. But, if it has nuts, chocolate, liqueur, coconut, pudding, and the right kind of fruit, you will probably wish to play through the end game.

Usually, there is time before dinner to reinforce your case. If you do not know who will be sitting to your right or left, you may wish to include, "I can't wait for dessert," among your witty banter before dinner, hoping someone who will eventually be sitting near you will hear. I must emphasize that there is no shame in this technique. If you suffer even a twinge of embarrassment at this stage of the ploy, you should give up the game immediately. The worst is yet to come.

If you have identified your closest dinner partners, you can home in on them and spare yourself the tiring process of telling as many people as you can that you are a dessert freak.

Having spread the word before dinner, you now enter the critical phase. As soon as is practical after you have taken your place at the table, you must say to your dinner partners to the right and left, and as loudly as possible, "May I have your dessert?" Or, "I'll trade you my broccoli for your dessert." You can lead up to it in many different ways. Use a preamble if you like in which you make references to your sweet tooth, chocoholism, deficient genes, whatever.

It can be especially productive if you can work an illness into it. I have never figured out what that illness might be, unless it's an addiction. In most of my strategies, I suggest that you usually can be successful if you get people to feel sorry for you. It can be applied to almost any situation.

One technique is to suggest that sweets are the only thing that settle an upset stomach. You must follow this seemingly innocuous comment with the knockout punch. A comment to the effect that the fish, or shrimp, or calzone, or artichoke hearts have made you feel slightly queasy, is almost a sure winner.

If you happen to be sitting next to someone who is on the slender side, make much of it. Suggest that they must be of strong will to deny themselves fattening foods. This flattery, and pride, will sometimes coerce them into forgoing dessert, unless of course their weight is the product of an enviable metabolism.

If the person next to you is overweight, you might suggest as tactfully as possible that they should skip the dessert. A mention of heart disease and/or diabetes will frequently frighten them and create what I call an "anomaly of the portly." It occasionally causes them to give up their dessert. Generally, however, you must remember what made them overweight in the first place. The "anomaly of the portly" is not epidemic.

I have actually known people who have feigned a fatal illness and make much of the fact that life's simple pleasures are all that remain for them. It's a winner. The downside is that from the moment people give you their dessert, they wait for you to die. Some do so impatiently if they have turned over a very special dessert to you.

One or two references, such as, "Where's the dessert?" during dinner tend to reinforce your case. Usually, by the time dessert arrives, someone is willing to make the sacrifice you desire if for no reason other than to shut you up.

It should be emphasized that you can use any or all of these ploys, or any combination thereof. It is my desire to merely point out opportunities available to you.

My most successful clients are those who use my strategies only as a starting point. You can tailor the recommendations to your own special talents or to the existing situation. As I'm sure you have noticed during the course of your social life, no two social events are exactly alike. Parties are like fingerprints and DNA.

We all have them, but no amount of planning can duplicate a past success or guarantee against repeating a dismal failure.

Having used any or all of the techniques I have proposed, the actual serving of the dessert determines one's success. "Oh, boy, finally!" is a favored comment upon arrival of the delicacy. It is a frisky reminder of your predilection. This is the critical moment. If the host or hostess has been alert, a second dessert will be served to you with the first. But this will occur only if there is a surplus. If you are served a single portion, immediately scan the table for any signs of people who have not taken spoon or fork to their plate. You can approach them later.

Your most likely target would be the person to your immediate right or left. A robust, "Are you going to eat your dessert?" is not out of line. "May I have that?" is another more aggressive way to put it.

I have found that if the early stages of the strategy are employed correctly, the chance of receiving a second dessert is in the vicinity of 82 percent. Statistically, there is a 66 percent probability of someone offering a third. Your chances are less than one in two of receiving a fourth.

Now, there is also a tactic for actually accepting the extra dessert. When the desired plate is proffered, take it firmly between the thumb and index finger and remove it from the grasp of the offering party. At this point, when it is impossible for them to deny you, simply say, "Oh, I couldn't." Then add quickly, "But, thank you. If you can't manage it, I'll do my best to see to it that it won't go to waste."

If you have used the sickness ploy, and believe that's why you are being offered the extra portion, it is a reassuring touch to add, "I feel much better now." Or a simple, "Bless you," can be very effective.

Chapter 2

Passing the Bread

It is difficult for some to remember which way to pass the bread or rolls at the dinner table. At home, it usually doesn't matter. Junior will reach into the next county for a hot biscuit, while most of us will just pass the basket toward its intended target in the most expeditious and efficient manner.

At a fancy dinner party, it is altogether another matter. Eyes will be raised, subtle winks passed, and elbows dug into a partner's ribs when some clod passes the rolls to the right (or is it left?).

On such occasions it is entirely possible for the mind to go blank. A guest at the other end of the table asks for "a roll please." When the rolls are directly in front of you, the mind turns to mush. It is wise to be prepared rather than to be embarrassed.

I always throw the rolls. Yes, throw them. I remember a place near Sikeston, Missouri, in which the specialty of the house is "throwed rolls." The happy host wanders through the dining room tossing warm rolls and biscuits at appreciative customers. I've never heard a customer complain. So, the next time you are faced with the dilemma at an elegant dinner party, simply take a roll from the basket and toss it at the claimant. He or she will usually look startled, often with amusing results. But, as you toss the roll, let out a resounding chuckle or whoop and tell the story of the restaurant and the "throwed rolls."

Believe me, it is a guaranteed winner. You'd better look up Sikeston in an atlas, by the way. After pulling this one off, you don't want to be tripped up by not knowing where it is.

Here is an additional strategy that my friend—with an eye for the ladies—developed. He would always look among the dinner guests for an attractive, well-endowed young woman wearing a low-cut gown.

As an amusing diversion he would seek an opportunity to "pass" her a roll. He always made certain the toss was short of the mark forcing her to bend forward to make the catch, often with pleasing results.

He insists the technique is a certain crowd pleaser among the men at the table, some of whom may try it themselves during the evening. One woman, who was a particularly attractive target at a recent dinner, was heard to say during dessert that she felt for a while as if she were dining in Baghdad.

CHAPTER 3

When a Friend or Acquaintance Introduces a Baby

I must emphasize at the very outset that I believe all babies, regardless of sex, look like either Edward G. Robinson, Winston Churchill, or Nikita Khrushchev. They continue to look that way for months, so it is extremely difficult for me to become wildly enthusiastic about what an infant looks like for several months, and in some cases, years.

However, as certainly as the swallows come back to Capistrano, as surely as the sun rises in the East, and as predictably as you will ever remain a *Powerball* loser, the parents of a newborn will expect compliments and all manner of enthusiasm directed at their new child. It has nothing to do with friendship.

This can become tedious. If the infant were simply waved at you like a flag and then taken someplace else for feeding, rest, or diaper changing, there would be no problem. We all know, however, it does not work that way. New parents usually feel duty-bound to subject friends, acquaintances, and even strangers to a prolonged first meeting with baby. Invariably, they will overstay their welcome. However, the true friend will never let on that a voice inside is screaming for the parent to "get that kid out of here!"

The scenario I hate the worst is the office visit, although it does present one with some advantages. For instance, you get to share your time with baby with the rest of the office staff. However, there is nothing worse than seeing Millie from accounting or Harold from the mail room heading into the workplace with a tiny blue or pink bundle.

Invariably, they time the arrival to coincide with your busiest day. I think I can safely say that no child has ever been brought to my office on a day other than one in which I am seeking to meet an impossible deadline. Fifty things are going on. Your desk phone and BlackBerry compete with e-mail and the fax machine. Couriers are coming and going. Bosses are haranguing you. Yet, in the moment of peak frenzy, a beaming Millie (from accounting, I think) stands in the doorway presenting herself, and baby, to staffers unlucky enough not to have been someplace else at the time.

Women are usually the first to respond. They shriek and giggle and head for the infant, eager to play with its fingers and pinch its cheeks to prove they still possess active maternal instincts. Men's shoulders slump. They know there is a ritual about to be performed from which there is little opportunity to escape in spite of the overwhelming desire to flee.

Often the child is asleep on arrival, but that cannot last long under such an assault. Within seconds it is crying, and everyone is ooohing and aaahing. "Isn't *it* cute," are the only decipherable words, unless someone actually knows the mother well enough to offer that "*it*" is a "he" or "she."

Then all play the game of pass the baby, which is certain to prolong the crying. First one woman then the next takes it, holds it, hugs it, and says something like, "It almost makes me want to have another." The baby is then quickly bounced into another pair of clutching hands.

And what is it about proximity to babies that inspires, nay forces, people to speak in baby talk? Men and women react as if the air in the room had been replaced by helium. Tone and timbre change. Grown people risk ridicule as they take on guttural incantations with the sole objective of eliciting a favorable reaction from the tiny treasure.

Sooner or later, the men feel obligated to pay their respects. Most do, except for those who were fortunate enough to see the scene developing early on and managed a quick exit. One by one they file by, pretend interest, and then say something inane. For reasons I do not understand, the entire drama must be played with a wide smile. Everyone (except baby) feels obligated to smile all the time.

This presents a certain irony, because mommy seems to spend a lot of her time pleading with the baby to smile so all might see that he or she is truly adorable.

"She has Pete's smile," someone will say, if indeed, the infant does manage even the slightest change in expression.

"It's Pete's smile, all right," mommy will offer, usually adding, "but she has MY hair."

And, so it goes, usually for an hour or more. I have seen occasions, however, in which mommy and baby are still there, waiting for even more attention, while the office staff is preparing to leave for the day and lights are being turned off. It is a horrid experience.

But none is worse than being summoned to the new parents' home. It requires valuable time from your day. It requires a gift. And holding the requisite smile for one or two or even three hours can be downright strenuous.

The biggest problem, of course, is that guests are a captive audience. Some families with a flair for the dramatic will let the entire production drag out interminably. The worst of these cases is when baby is asleep when you arrive. That means you have to tiptoe into a room festooned with baby things like stuffed animals, dolls, mobiles, music boxes, and colorful quilts. The inevitable economy-sized box of Pampers is always somewhere close by. In the midst of it all is baby.

You slink by saying something obligatory, hoping the baby will wake up soon so you can get the whole thing over with. Mommy then ensures a lengthy visit by inviting you for coffee and cake while waiting for baby's hunger to waken it.

It will, and does. And, if you are lucky, it will not require a wait longer than one cup of coffee and two pieces of cake. It is during this time that the gifts are presented and you realize your jaws and cheeks hurt from constant smiling.

There is no doubt when baby finally wakens. Your first inclination is to comment on the strength of its lungs; however, you realize in time that this family has one of those intercom gadgets that enables parents in the living room to hear every snort and wheeze from baby while it sleeps. Moments later it is brought triumphantly into the living room.

The next concern is how baby will be fed. That it will be fed there can be no doubt. And that it will be fed before your very eyes is not debatable. The question is, will it get a bottle or mommy's ample breast. I still feel uncomfortable being present during breast feeding. I should be over it by now because it is increasingly the style as more and more mommies are nursing, frequently in public. I am not, however.

Eventually, the satiation process is completed. It is at this point that things get dicey. Now, all guests are somehow expected to play with baby. It is never enough to simply carry on about the infant's cuteness, how much it looks like so and so, or how tempting it would be to have another. No. You must, at some point, actually touch the child. Usually, some well-meaning matron will suggest that you hold the tyke. You must be especially careful, especially after the child has just eaten.

When people take babies, they always hold it so its chin can rest on their shoulder. The problem is that you can't actually see baby's face in this position. It is bad form and tiring to hold it away from you at arm's length, even though this is the preferred method of most men. Invariably, it will get something on the one who holds it. At best, it will be a drop or two of spittle. If one is unlucky, it may drool a few ounces on the new sportsjacket. If one has been careless in handling baby, it might get messy.

Research indicates that babies being held by men will throw up 98.82 percent of the time on such occasions. Men should always put a towel or something between baby's head and that sport coat.

There is always the possibility, and perhaps even the probability, of a double whammy. That, of course, is baby throwing up, then depositing a disproportionately large load in its Pampers while it is still in the guest's possession.

Bad as it is, the true unpleasantness lies ahead. That, however, is more often a problem for the wife than for the man. Invariably, mommy will ask the woman to accompany her while she changes the diaper. From that point on the visit begins to wind down.

You can hasten the moment by commenting after the diaper change as to how tired the new mom looks. It's good for ten or fifteen minutes of discussion about the rigors of childbirth, but it does offer a nice opportunity to move toward departure. "You should get some rest," is a good start.

There are times, though I don't know why, in which some will actually invite the new family into their home. The only advantage to the invitation is that it is possible to pretend to be out of something at coffee time and offer to run to the store. One does have to come back, however, and this is good for only a short respite.

There is also the unannounced home visit, an especially dreadful phenomenon that should be prohibited by law or constitutional amendment.

The most remarkable aspect of the home visit, announced or otherwise, is the amount of paraphernalia that accompanies baby even for a short stay. There may be an unwritten rule of parenthood, and perhaps it goes back to our earliest ancestors, that when traveling with baby, it is necessary to bring along all of its possessions. It probably has its origins in an early nomadic culture. There are sacks and bags and blankets and cases. The amount rivals that of a family of four crossing the Atlantic on the *QE2*. In comes all the necessary trappings, wave after wave, to be piled high in some corner of a large room. About it all is the definite aroma of baby powder, which will linger in the house for days.

When baby appears, it is usually covered in blankets, sweaters, and layers of other garments that are peeled off onionlike. Once the child is finally revealed, the scenario is played out very much like the visit to the baby's own home.

The best that can be said for this type of visit is that you get what you deserve for having issued the invitation in the first place. The only advantage is that the host saves the time it would have taken to drive to visit baby in its own environs. Having the freedom to move about in one's own home also has advantages. But when all the pluses and minuses are added, it makes for a fairly miserable couple of hours, no matter where or when you are introduced to baby.

There is one exception. There is a best-case scenario, and there is also a means for avoiding any and all of the worst situations.

First, the best-case scenario. Few of us are fortunate enough to have a limited first encounter with a friend's or acquaintance's baby. There is something like an obligation first-time parents feel about presenting their baby to the world. That's why they return to the office, invite you to their home, or visit you in your home. It is an instinctive drive that has been unfavorably compared to the spawning of salmon.

Yet, much of the aforementioned ritual can be avoided if one is fortunate enough to meet baby in a chance encounter. It can be in a park, a mall, or a supermarket. No matter. The chance encounter requires no time. It requires no gift. No travel. No holding the baby. No changing the diaper. No vomit on one's collar. No spittle. All it really requires is something like, "Oh, is that the new baby? It sure is _____ [you fill in the blank]. Sorry, I've got to run." Then, run indeed. You get extra points if you had the presence of mind to suggest that mumps or swine flu has recently been a visitor to your home. It can preclude the surprise visit.

This brings me to a key point. What does one say when confronted by a new baby and new baby's parents? The infant could care less. With the parents, however, it is quite a different matter. As I indicated earlier, it is especially difficult for me to compliment a baby's looks because they all look pretty much like Robinson, Churchill, or Khrushchev. You certainly don't want to say, "Gee, she looks exactly like Edward G. Robinson."

You might gag saying the kid is cute or gorgeous or beautiful. It might even be an untimely comment, especially if something is running from the child's nose or if crusted throw up is visible on its chin.

It might be difficult to suggest the little darling looks like mom or dad, or grandma or grandpa. In fact, you may know none of the above. Many words may escape you.

There is one phrase, however, which will work very well, as long as baby is awake. You will never miss by saying, "My, he [or she] looks very alert." The beauty of the phrase is that it implies intelligence. Parents accept it willingly as not only a confirmation of what they already know, but also because it suggests a favorable reflection upon themselves.

The phrase works less well when baby is asleep. Fear not. All is not lost. In the chance encounter, or any other for that matter when baby is in a deep sleep, it works very nicely to suggest that the infant has a "fine disposition." Again, it confirms the type of perfection parents have already observed in their youngster. And it reflects nicely on the child's forbearers, first and foremost, its parents.

I call it the A and D premise. Awake, use alert; Deep sleep, use disposition.

Now, my final advice. The sad reality of life is that it will be difficult to avoid having to make do over someone else's baby. Whether it be the chance encounter, the unannounced office or home visit, sooner or later it will happen to you. My preferred method for minimizing contact with little ones is very simple. Whether during the office visit, when invited to the home stay, or during the supermarket chance encounter, simply say, "I'd love to get close to the little rascal, but I have this awful cold."

Chapter 4

How to Avoid Accepting an Unexpected Invitation, Even When You Don't Have Time to Think of a Good Excuse

We have all experienced times when we have been forced to accept an unwanted invitation even when the invite is to an event, or involves people, we abhor. We usually are trapped by the timing of an unexpected invitation.

There is something about people who issue such invitations. They seem to have an instinct for blindsiding us, coming at us out of the sun with all the cunning of a hawk swooping in on a helpless rabbit. Often the effect is much the same. We never know what hit us. If only I had thought of this, or that, we think later, I would not be dressed in this starched shirt and ugly tie heading for a religious symposium on Super Bowl Sunday.

The main problem is the unanticipated nature of the offensive invitation. The invite typically comes at an unusual time, or is issued by a person so far removed from your own social circle or with whom you have so little in common, that an invitation of any sort is the farthest thing from your mind.

Timing is an important ally to the assailant. He or she may not know it, but if the invitation comes totally out of context, or in some other non sequitur fashion, it can be devastating to the recipient.

I can remember being at my daughter's soccer practice one night, impatient to get her, and myself, home for dinner. A wisp of a man I had assumed on past occasions to be another parent approached me smiling. I smiled back. We watched as the kids were going through the final paces and we made small talk about it.

Thinking back on it, I should have seen it coming, but, as is so often the case, I did not. As we chatted, he said something like, "I'm glad to finally have the chance of meeting you. You are the only other father I have not met." I nodded and mumbled something.

He waited a moment, then said, "I hope you'll join the rest of us for our W.T.F.C. social next Sunday. Everyone else will be there."

Zap! I had been hit. My daughter was approaching us, flushed red with good exercise. "May I put you down?" the man pressed.

"Sunday?" I blurted. "What time?" I asked as my daughter was wiping her sweaty brow on my new suit jacket.

"Excellent. I was hoping you'd make it. I'll put you down," he said extracting an envelope from his jacket. "Two-o-clock," he said. "My place," he added, shoving the envelope into my hand. He rubbed my daughter on her head. "We're so happy to have your daddy with us," he said, smiling. With that, he turned and left, walking quickly.

I looked at the envelope. The bad feeling was starting.

"I didn't know you knew Pastor Richmand," said my daughter.

The bad feeling was getting worse.

"Pastor Richmand?" I asked. "Who is Pastor Richmand?"

"He's our host," said my daughter. "This is his field. He lets us practice here."

The feeling was really bad now. I looked at the envelope. The letters W.T.F.C. were emblazoned on the paper.

"What's W.T.F.C.?" I asked, certain my voice was shaking by now.

"Working Together for Christ," she responded cheerfully. "He's invited all the dads for a Christian workshop Sunday. He also wants to ask the fathers to help put some new grass on our field. He's sooo nice daddy. You'll like him." She squeezed my hand. "Can we go now? I'm hungry."

I saw some other fathers, clutching a child in one hand and an invitation in the other, walking to their cars. All of them . . . we . . . walked with slumped shoulders. We had all been snookered. Sunday was the day of the Dallas–San Francisco game. Ouch. And we'd be spending it Working Together for Christ AND sodding an enormous soccer field.

There is also something slightly coercive about such invitations. None more so than the invitation from a boss. I was riding in the office elevator one day after I had picked up a copy of Jean-Paul Sartre's *Being and Nothingness* for my college sophomore son during my lunch hour. I was leafing through it when Mr. W. W. Otis Nixon, the president and CEO of my company, entered the elevator. He is a gentleman who is as imposing as he is powerful and, as I was to learn, impulsive.

We exchanged greetings. Later that afternoon I received a note from Nixon. It read in part: "I noticed your preference for philosophy in the elevator. Please join me tomorrow (a Saturday) at 3:00 at the Wabash Athletic Club Reading Room. My philosophy reading and discussion group is meeting, and I'm sure you'll enjoy our discourse."

The range of my emotions was rather broad, bounded on the one side by my desire to get ahead in the company, and, on the other, by my overwhelming fear of any discussion remotely associated with philosophy, or any subject considered remotely intellectual. I did know instantly, however, that I wanted to be anyplace but the Wabash A.C. that Saturday afternoon. But I was trapped.

W. W. Nixon had done it one way. Pastor Richmand, another.

Had I known then what I know now, I would have avoided that disastrous Sunday with the pastor. I would have seen Dallas take San Francisco into sudden-death overtime for a dramatic victory. And I would have dodged the unbearably boring Saturday discussion at the Wabash A.C. My boss did not participate, by the way. He had been called to New York to discuss what turned out to be a big merger and an even bigger golden parachute.

My strategy for avoiding these invitations, and others like them, is very simple. However, it involves one component that must be adhered to always. You must be prepared to employ it instantly when the offensive invitation is given. To delay for any length of time is to suggest that you have fabricated an excuse. My philosophy is not that fabrication is bad, it is that making that fabrication APPEAR to be a fabrication is bad.

So, you must have your response so ingrained, so automatic, and so spontaneous that it comes out as naturally as your very breath.

Your response must also meet certain criteria. It must apply to any invitation issued for any time of day or night. It must also be plausible enough so that the little girl hanging on your arm after soccer practice will accept it without embarrassing comment. By the way, it also should have the advantage of enabling you to change your mind later in the unlikely event you would want to.

And what is that response?

"I'd love to, but I'm having elective surgery. Nothing serious; however, the doctors want me to stay put for twelve to twenty-four hours."

If, as in the case of my invitation at the soccer field, a child or even a spouse is with you, you must be ready. If you sense trouble from either, you may say that you hadn't mentioned it because you didn't want to cause any alarm. It has the nifty residue effect of making people feel sorry for you.

In any case, the "nothing serious" should assuage any concerns.

CHAPTER 5

Inviting People to Parties Knowing They Can't Come

My wife and I are not social outcasts. We are "homers." We have kids. We don't go out much. We enjoy staying at home. We enjoy going out, too, but only after we have complained about having to go. Once we are wherever it is we have been invited to go, we usually enjoy ourselves.

One reason we blanch at invitations is we know that sooner or later we'll have to respond in kind. Usually, it's later. We don't like to give parties. I don't like it because I usually feel I have to lay in enough liquor to bathe an army. That's costly. And all by myself, I usually finish drinking the vast reservoirs left over at just about the time we plan our next party.

My wife hates to entertain because she feels compelled to clean the house—not just clean it, sterilize it! Her greatest fear is that a speck of dust will be spotted, noted, and used against her at some future date, with or without her direct knowledge. She dreads being accused in gossip of being a careless housekeeper.

So, our happy compromise is to build up a fistful of social IOUs, then pretty much ignore them for as long as we can. However, we have struck upon a happy method of dealing with our guilt.

We employ techniques not unfamiliar to the CIA, the FBI, or the intelligence unit of the local police department. We listen, we watch, we wait, and we keep good notes about our friends and important dates in their lives.

Here's how it works. First, you buy some very expensive invitations. You make a list of people you owe. Then, the waiting game begins. What you are waiting for is information about people on that list. Information on their travel plans. That's right. You wait to hear that Fred and Wilma are going to Palm Springs for a week. Having learned they are leaving town, you must be very careful to determine exactly when they will be away. This information is usually fairly easily obtained because in all probability you move in the same circles.

"RECEIVING AN INVITATION"

Once the date has been determined, it is no trick at all to take one of those expensive invitations, pick a party date on which you know they'll be out of town, and invite them. They'll have to regret, of course, and if you play your cards correctly, you can sometimes exact a small measure of guilt from the departing couple by saying something like, "You always leave town just when we have a party."

There are those happy occasions, too, when you learn that several couples may be going out of town together. It is good form to send invitations to all. This accomplishes many things. The group will speak kindly of you on the trip. You will have maintained the all-important social *quid pro quo*. And you may not even owe some of those making the trip. That means they will feel obligated to invite you to their next party. You can decline in comfort, knowing you cannot be criticized for finding an excuse to decline when they failed to attend your mythical bash.

My wife and I usually feel the social slate has been wiped clean when we have sent two unaccepted invitations for each event for which we feel we owe.

There are some dangers in this technique, of course, although it is clearly worth the risk. There is always a hazard that the departing couple, or couples, will mention to some of your other friends that they are going to miss your party. Only the rudest of your acquaintances would confront you about your failure to invite them. In the unhappy event that happens, you can invite them and actually throw a party.

Or, and this is my favorite, you can express your disappointment that Fred and Wilma mentioned it, saying that what you were really doing was setting up a surprise party for the rude, offended friend. This is where good intelligence comes in. If they should ask why, it would be good to know the date of their birthdays or anniversary, or otherwise tie it into an event in their lives. When trapped with no such convenient dates, just say that you were planning the surprise simply to say thanks for being such a good friend all these years, months, weeks, days, or whatever. You can go on to explain that now that the surprise is out of the bag, you'll just have to do it another time, probably after Fred and Wilma return.

Chapter 6

Excuses for Not Going Someplace You Don't Want to Go

The fertile mind is the preserve of all excuses. There is unbounded opportunity here. Let me begin by saying what not to do: Never make an excuse that can be effectively challenged or that can be proven to be a lie.

My wife has the facile mind. However, she lacks one talent. She will tell a neighbor she cannot accompany her shopping by blurting out that it is our daughter's birthday. Not a bad excuse for someone who lives in the next county.

However, with the neighbor lady coming and going, we have to cover ourselves by creating the illusion that there's a party going on at our place. Horror of horrors, this usually means having to actually invite other children onto the property. Sometimes, it also requires tying balloons on the front porch to give a festive impression.

Even this ruse is better than her rejecting an invitation from friends by saying I am busy catching up on yard work. There is only one way to counter that one! My wife once told friends I had a horrible virus. I was unable to play golf for the entire weekend. I've never forgiven her.

Now, here is a list of winning excuses for all occasions. As I've mentioned, you are limited only by restrictions on your imagination. Tip: A certain degree of improbability always adds to the authenticity of your excuse. For instance, "my mother is sick" pales in comparison to "I am awaiting a phone call from Hillary Clinton."

Here goes: It is your day for volunteering at the AIDS clinic. This is especially effective if you are rejecting an invitation from someone you never want to hear from again. Few will visit the clinic to check out your story.

You have a possible diagnosis of hepatitis.

You are being interviewed later in the day by the FBI concerning an acquaintance who may be nominated for a big government job.

You have been requested to take part in a police lineup because you resemble a suspect.

You are going on a church retreat.

The Red Cross has just called for an emergency donation of your very rare blood type.

You have volunteered to clean up following a Greek party at your church, son's school, country club, or fraternal organization.

You are attending a meeting of parents, parishioners, or country club members to discuss the disclosure that a teacher, pastor, or chef is one of the Mariel boat people.

You are awaiting results of tests to determine if your dog or cat has rabies.

You can't stop throwing up.

And so it goes. As you have probably noticed, the best excuses preclude the probability that the people to whom you are giving the excuse will drop by to check.

Once, my wife used the hepatitis line on a friend. We found a pot of chicken soup on the front porch the next morning. Our friends left it without even ringing the doorbell.

CHAPTER 7

Leaving a Party

Why is it so difficult to leave a party? Especially a boring one. Presumably, it's because the polite guest wishes to give no offense.

Nonetheless, as the evening drags on and you become more impatient to leave, it can be difficult. No one wants to be the first to depart. Not only does it give the impression you are not grateful, but others may talk about you when you are gone. Most impatient guests choose to wait for a first couple to leave. However, because no one wants to be the first pair out, everyone stays lots longer than they wanted.

This can lead to another difficult period. There are times when a first couple opens the exit floodgate. When that brazen pair announces the intention to depart, everyone else does the same. Almost everyone else. You must be very alert to this situation. If you miss that wave, you can be stuck for an indeterminate amount of time afterwards, because (1) you again do not wish to give offense, and (2) you do not wish to give an impression that you are subject to a herd instinct. Frankly, if you have gotten yourself into a situation where you are the last guests left at a party, you have only yourself to blame. All the more reason to carry a PED, Personal Electronic Device. Yes, putting the popularity of today's technology to work maximizes its value.

This is the most effective means available for a quick, unexpected, and, if it's your desire, premature departure. (This is handy if you have two parties to attend on the same night, or if you're just plain bored.) Doctors have been using this technique for years. Now that vibrating devices are omnipresent, you do not need an accomplice to actually make the call.

Years ago, before cell phones, a friend of mine used to pay his young daughter to call him at a prearranged time. She would call, scream her father's or mother's name and babble incoherently, sobbing all the while. Mom or dad would take the call, announce an emergency, and leave immediately. The child supplemented her allowance nicely, and the parents were usually the first ones home from parties, seminars, Tupper Ware gatherings, or church socials. Now, of course, the call can be made by one's partner from the water closet.

The downside, of course, is that this technique can usually withstand only one pass through one's circle of friends. To try this twice on the same host or hostess can lead to much damaging gossip. My friends were forced to stop it when one of their neighbors, hearing the girl's screaming into the phone, filed an anonymous charge of child abuse. The cops came. It was nasty.

Using the PED is much safer. And when you no longer have to pay an accomplice, expensive gadgets can quickly pay for themselves. In fact, you don't even need the real thing if you can find a nice replica.

Here's how to do it. Make certain everyone is aware you are carrying such equipment. Checking e-mail occasionally works nicely, as does an infrequent text or tweet. I suggest keeping your jacket open during the evening to show the holstered device. A hands-on-hips swagger will help. Women should carry the equipment in their purses and, at least once during the evening, should interrupt a conversation (preferably with the host or hostess), by checking the device and pretending to read a message. Then, and this is a nice touch, disregard it. You might say something chic like, "Damned leash. I don't know why I continue to carry this thing.

It's more a nuisance than anything." I find the dinner table is a good place to perform this charade. Everyone is brought into the deception at one time.

This incident does two things. It establishes the fact that you have the electronic equipment. And it establishes the fact it is vibrating equipment. It is for this reason I suggest you carry the real McCoy. Sometimes a guest who is not initiated in the world of high technology will insist on your activating the device to demonstrate the vibrator. (I have a nice joke I usually use in this circumstance, however, it is too crude for these pages.)

Then, at the critical time, you simply unveil your device and say something like, "Oh my God." Call any number you wish. Your own number works quite nicely, although there is always a risk your child or babysitter will answer, requiring a real conversation.

The best number to call is your own device phone number. It will ring busy, but give you all the time you need for an imaginary emergency conversation.

From that point, it is all downhill. You can let your imagination take over. "Of course, I'll be there immediately," is more than sufficient and elegant in its simplicity if your host or hostess is within earshot. If they are not, simply go to them, say the word, *emergency*, and let your, and their, imagination be the guide for the rest of it.

Invariably, the caring host or hostess will ask if there is anything they can do. Wave them off and leave, shouting, "No. Thanks for the offer. I'll explain later."

 A word of caution. Sometimes those who play this exciting game can get carried away with the very drama of it. When you do leave, don't forget to bring your partner. Failure to do so can lead to a very difficult time.

And in the event some well-meaning soul at the gathering offers to bring your spouse home, you must blunt this effort immediately. After all, in all likelihood, you intend to be home lounging in comfortable clothes. You certainly don't want to wait in the dark until your partner is ferried home—especially an angry partner who had wanted to depart just as eagerly as you.

So, if someone makes that offer, say something like, "Thanks, but this emergency requires us both." Or you may shriek, "The call was for her!" A nice touch is for both of you to run from the building together, hand in hand.

This method is especially good for departing all boring, or otherwise tedious, occasions. If you have ever accepted an invitation to attend one of those business or assertiveness training seminars, this technique is quite handy. It also works nicely at business, religious, or social consciousness retreats. However, if you have agreed beforehand to attend such events, you should be made to pay the price.

This ploy is also very effective at ducking out of most wedding receptions, Bar Mitzvah's, any professional command performance, occasions with most relatives, church socials, or the periodic school function. It is especially useful for events hosted by boring acquaintances, who captured you because the invitation was unexpected and you did not have time to think of an acceptable excuse.

CHAPTER 8

When Your Dog Violates a Neighbor's Lawn

This is embarrassing, and rightly so. Your neighbor has a right to be angry, and you can't always control where Fido does his or her business. No matter that the dog has been hitting the same spot for as long as you've had it, you don't like to be caught in the act, even if it is the dog's act.

To begin with, if the neighbor sees it happen, there is no denying it. The problem then is getting out of the embarrassing situation with as little embarrassment as possible. If you can embarrass the neighbor at the same time, all the better.

If you are like most dog owners, you do not like walking with a pooper scooper. Chances are you don't even own one. Plastic bags or gloves make for especially nasty cleanup. Then there's the equally distasteful problem of what to do with the poop after it's been scooped.

Let me be perfectly clear about this: I do not advocate walking with the dog—ever! Take your chances with local leash laws and difficult neighbors by letting the dog run free, do its business wherever it likes, and in private, and come home when it will. This gives you a full array of excuses. You can say the dog got out when the kids left the door open, that your wife was run over by a car when she was walking the dog, or that it got away from you chasing a raccoon from the neighbor's trash, good neighbor that you are. This is one of my favorites. And, if from time to time your dog has tipped a neighbor's garbage can looking for an irresistible piece of bad meat, the neighbor will assume the raccoons are the problem. Yes, I like this one.

At some point, however, a red-faced neighbor may come to your door with a complaint about your dog soiling his yard.

The best ploy is to proclaim great joy. "Thank God," you may bellow. "He's been constipated, and doctors said Fido would have to undergo expensive surgery. It may be a parasite. Let me collect his stool, and take it to the doctor right away." Unfortunately, this does require you to collect the stool. Small price to pay for the privilege of allowing your dog to run free.

You might add, just to try giving the neighbor a bit of a guilt trip, "Fido has not been himself lately," and might go so far as to suggest another neighbor has apparently been putting out poison to discourage those pesky raccoons, and that your dog may have ingested some, causing doggie incontinence.

The problems begin the second time it happens. This is where your mettle is tested to the extreme. You can suggest that your dog has a "free range license" because of its breed (and hope the neighbor buys into that with no further investigation). Or, my favorite is to ask the neighbor if he/she would be willing to "go halfies" on a chain-link fence to contain the dog. Be certain to specify "chain link." Few in the neighborhood will be enthusiastic about construction of this unsightly barrier much less agree to pay for half of it. Your neighbor may surprise you by announcing that he will build a fence of his own (probably not chain link) to keep your animal at bay. Could there be a more perfect solution?

By the way, one good ploy is to try and place the blame for your bad dog on your neighbor's kids. You can gain quick advantage by suggesting the kids have been taunting your animal, and that it has encouraged irregular behavior. If you feel any sense of advantage at all, say you're not happy about it. If the neighbor suffers from one grain of paranoia, this may be interpreted as prelude to a lawsuit. If so, he is not likely to complain again soon.

If your dog is caught time and time again and you begin to run out of excuses, you may have to (1) let the animal out only in darkness, (2) walk it in another neighborhood, or (3) move.

Chapter 9

How to Insult People in Ways That Make You Feel Good and That Make Them Believe Is a Compliment

Let's face it, there are times when we have to suck it up and congratulate someone when it is the very last thing we wish to do. It may be a boss, a colleague, an old boyfriend of the wife, a former high school rival, or even a blood relative. It may come on occasions when compliments are undeserved but nonetheless bestowed.

The most dramatic example I can think of came when I was a child. A swimmer almost drowned off a crowded New Jersey beach. He had been caught in the undertow. A young lout, whose name has long since been lost to me, was also caught in the undertow. I watched the whole episode unfold. First, the trapped swimmer was whisked to sea. He began flailing and shouting, and otherwise trying to attract attention. Not being a good swimmer myself, I hurried to lifeguards. At this point, other bathers were becoming aware of the situation. As I got to the guards, I noticed another swimmer being whisked out to sea in the same direction as the first unfortunate. He reached the first swimmer quickly and reached for him urgently. It looked to many as if he was trying to keep the original swimmer from going under.

However, I could see the new panic in the face of the first swimmer who seemed locked in a life-or-death struggle to get out of the second man's grasp. "Save him, save him," shouted people from the beach. I was incredulous, because it had been clear to me from the outset that the second individual had also been caught in the undertow and was swept out to the first man.

Nonetheless, to a man, woman, and child, everyone on the beach assumed swimmer number two was actually attempting to rescue the first man. Even the lifeguards were perceptibly slowed by the drama. They did swing into action eventually, and effected a very nice rescue by boat. I don't know what was said on the boat, but the second swimmer had either been told, or was perceptive

enough to understand, that he was being regarded as some kind of hero.

When the boat broke from the surf, the crowd cheered. The original undertow victim was too scared to care or attempt denials. He jumped from the boat and immediately began puking his guts out at the edge of the surf. But the crowd's attention was on the second swimmer. People all but lifted him to their shoulders in praise and began chanting, "Hero, hero, hero." He beamed at the reaction.

I took one look at the first swimmer, who was all but ignored by the mob. I could see in his expression that he wondered why this person who had almost drowned him while trying to save himself was being singled out for praise. He was clearly more grateful to be alive than he was in setting the record straight, so he turned and walked up the beach, away from the crowd, stopping every few steps to retch.

We, and the faux hero, were the only people on the beach who knew what had really happened. It was then that I made a remark that was to set the tone for every undeserved compliment I was ever to give again. I walked up to the newly crowned hero and said, "That was an incredible example of courage. Rarely, have I seen it in such an extreme." My eyes locked on his. At that moment, I knew that he knew that I knew.

No, he did not break down and confess to the mob. After swallowing hard, he looked at me, smiled, and turned back to accept more compliments. Nonetheless, I felt better. (Here I must confess that had I been asked to advise this young man on how to act in these circumstances, I would have suggested he do nothing differently.)

The point, in case you have missed it, is this: some lovely words used in certain ways have a subtle double meaning.

Is an "incredible" performance necessarily a good one?

Is an "extraordinary" event by definition exemplary?

If you have given a "remarkable" speech, was it a fine speech?

A person can be "unique," but that does not imply a quality person. Mother Teresa is one of a kind, but so were Hitler, Stalin, and Charles Manson.

Get my point? Tell your wife that you believe her cooking is "singular," or that her garish costume is "inventive." Tell your boss that he is "without peer." Tell the guy who stole your high school sweetheart that you have "thought of him often over the years." You need not say that every recollection included a particularly heinous form of homicide.

And, as for that sweetheart, tell her that she still occupies a "special place" in your dreams. Simply calling someone "special" has its own charm. When you are forced by circumstance into making a tribute, you might try saying, "I just can't find the words to tell you what I think."

You can be as inventive as you like. While you may not have quite the satisfaction of just telling someone off, it can be gratifying to know that your compliment has a nice edge to it—a double edge. Half a loaf is better than none.

A fun pastime is adding to the list. Try it while driving, raking the leaves, or standing in line at the supermarket. And, if that line is moving slowly, you can practice by telling the cashier she is "one of a kind."

They work very nicely if you are satisfied insulting someone who does not get the slur. If you want the satisfaction of knowing that the target realizes he is the object of a verbal assault, there is a long list of simpler words that will fill the bill. I'm afraid, however, you'll have to look elsewhere for them. This is a family publication.

Chapter 10

Excuses and Other Strategies for Passing Wind

Some of the very best and very worst moments in life involve the fart.

Its legend and lore is recorded through the ages. Farts have been embarrassing people for centuries. There is a story in *1,001 Arabian Nights* about a poor soul who left a village in disgrace after passing a particularly horrendous wind. He waited a number of years before summoning the courage to return. As he walked back into the village, he heard a young boy ask the lad's mother in what year he had been born. It was to the man's horror that he heard her reply, "You were born the year El Hashish (or whatever his name was) farted."

There are stories of lesser and greater magnitude. Flatulence happens. What I plan to address here is what to do when it happens to you.

First and foremost, if it happens when you are alone, don't worry about it. Most people won't admit it, but they kind of enjoy their own farts. When it happens when you are in the company of others, or when someone unexpectedly walks into a room after you have indulged, that's when the problems begin. So, let us go to work.

There are three basic situations. The need to fart. The accidental fart. And covering the fart. At times there is very little distinction between them. It is advisable to learn how to segue between them.

The need to fart is a direct cousin to accidental flatulence, and is familiar to us all. However, once realized, it can be dodgy. Circumstances such as one's environment, uncertainty as to what form the actual emission will take, and one's relative proximity to empathetic companions, or potentially hostile strangers, will dictate the course of action. This is complicated by the fact that there are occasions when the actual flatulence precedes one's knowledge of the need. That would be the accidental fart, which will be covered later. All emissions will likely require cover.

Let me be clear that once the need to fart is realized it is important to deal with it quickly lest one suffer some gastro-intestinal discomfort. The longer one resists, the greater the likelihood that the discomfort will evolve into intolerable pain. That can result in the reckless "I don't give a damn fart" in which the instigator ignores the consequences of the transgression. In such cases, all caution is . . . you should pardon the expression . . . thrown to the wind. Such intentional recklessness usually results in the perpetrator's immediate discovery in which he or she will inevitably be ridiculed, censured, and/or ostracized. Anyone who submits to this temptation deserves whatever consequences follow.

The decision as to pass wind or not (if a decision is even involved) can be further complicated by not knowing whether the oncoming flatulence will be noisy or silent. The latter is commonly referred to as the "silent but deadly" (SBD) variety. Each is risky.

Under the most favorable conditions, one will find oneself near a handy restroom in which to find private relief. The British normally refer to such a sanctuary as a Water Closet or WC. Until recently I always thought that WC was British shorthand for "Wind

Cabin" or "Wind Control." Finding this protective shelter from humiliation is almost too much to ask for. Other possible dodges, if available, may include standing near . . . cooking food (preferably cabbage) . . . a pet . . . a homeless person . . . any of which, with careful positioning, can deflect responsibility nicely. Good luck.

We all know that life does not work that way. That is why I am offering the following suggestions. It is my hope they will encourage you to pre-plan so, at best, you can dodge one of life's embarrassing situations, or, at worst, shift the blame elsewhere. We cannot cover all circumstances here, but when you feel the need to or actually emit, the following advice should help you meet the crisis.

The accidental fart can be quite humorous or quite embarrassing. It depends largely on your audience. It is quite different to cut one at the frat house than it is to let one rip at the boss's dinner party.

We've all experienced the accidental fart. They pop up during a laugh or while coughing, and sometimes even during a sigh. Sometimes they are quite loud, and other times they slip out all but unnoticed. At first! Remember that in every circumstance, covering the emission is the primary mission.

The trick with the accidental fart, as with all farts, is to disassociate oneself with the deed as quickly as possible. Proximity can be an indictment. Distance a reprieve. It is easier to slip away, of course, if you have cut one of the silent ones. Move smartly. If outside, it is advisable to be aware of wind conditions at all times. Place yourself downwind from companions. Find an open window if you are inside. Standing beneath a whirring ceiling fan also works. You must distance yourself from the deed and the ultimate odor by whatever means possible. Speed is, you will pardon the expression, of the essence. It is also advisable to practice facial and verbal expressions of disdain. (See covering the fart.)

What has just been covered is the easiest of all flatulence with which to distance oneself. More problematical is the fart that is both deliberate (or accidental) and loud.

Again, one must always be aware of one's environment. A loud fart will be received differently at a rock concert than it will be at a funeral. At the rock concert, you are essentially home free. A report comparable to that left behind by the *Enola Gay* will go quite unnoticed at most rock concerts. At a Sarah Brightman concert, it is quite a different story. However, at a funeral, one must be most clever indeed. The trick here is to accomplish disassociation, and put distance between oneself, the act, and its consequences. Farting apparently happens a lot in church. Some think it may have inspired the word *pew*.

Perpetrators must be quite alert. At the instant of the report, it must be sized up immediately and analyzed for sound. I put the sounds into two categories: the kazoo and the explosion. Experts would refine the sound into a thousand categories. Fact is, it is either high pitched or what I call rumble pitched.

Therefore, at a funeral, and in most circumstances, you can react in one of two ways. The kazoo sound usually is matched nicely with high-pitched wailing, or even sobbing. Arab women have an interesting technique called keening. It is achieved by wailing and by clicking the tongue against the roof of the mouth. A high-pitched cry is always a good cover at a funeral. I have never figured out if keening is an expression of true emotion or whether Arab women fart a lot at funerals.

Of course, you'll want to leave the scene quickly. Sobbing and leaving the funeral ceremony hastily and unexpectedly is not inconsistent with the funeral ambience. My advice is to leave the church, cemetery, or funeral parlor, proceed directly to the car, then leave the area altogether. The fart residue may remain behind, but you are gone and disassociated from the deed entirely.

The technique for the rumble fart is similar. Instead of keening, however, I recommend coughing. One can duplicate most rumble sounds with imaginative coughing. Again, one is not surprised to see someone with a bad cough leave a public gathering. Again, I recommend getting as far away from the area as quickly as possible to completely disassociate yourself from the residue.

These techniques actually work very well in most circumstances. If the mishap occurs at the boss's party, it may be difficult to leave the house and drive away. If you are trapped among a group of guests one of two feints may be helpful. Once the odor is detected, make a face showing some level of discomfort and disdain. You will surely join the others in this response. Failure to do so will likely single you out as the perpetrator. Glancing in an accusing manner at any member of the group is helpful in raising doubt as to the source of the irritant. Making quickly for the WC can sometimes work, if you don't mind risking the ridicule of others during your absence if, as is likely to be the case, your perfidy is assumed.

You may have to make do with other devices. A kazoo fart at the dinner table can be countered with a sharp "whoop!" You can proclaim that the potato was too hot, or, if it occurs during dessert, that the sorbet was surprisingly cold. Don't worry about offending the hostess. She would much rather think you had burned your tongue than think you had farted.

Now, as to the residue, and this applies in an SBD situation as well, quick thinking is everything. Waving one's napkin and proclaiming, "Gee it's hot in here," can sometimes work. Following that with blowing out a candle, apologizing for ruining the ambience, then relighting it immediately can be a nifty technique if you are athletically inclined. The lighted match will consume many of the residue gasses. Keep in mind, however, that you are drawing attention to yourself and the contaminated area.

There are other ploys. You can push your plate off the table, spill your water or wine glass, or simply inquire innocently as to whether the hosts have a dog. Then, pray they do. A dog can be a Godsend. Remember, a fart can always be attributed to a nearby

dog. If a dog remains under the table during the dinner, where they sometimes are sleeping or awaiting crumbs, you can forget all other strategies. The very strong of heart (sometimes called the Strongheart ploy) can pass a considerable volume of gas and then proclaim indignantly, "Damn dog!" The pet's proximity gives the flatulence-prone guest free rein to blast away at will. The dog will always be blamed.

Finally, especially when all assembled are close friends—members of a card club or a softball team perhaps—or when all else is lost and you need to deflect blame, you can always ask the time-honored question, "Who farted?"

CHAPTER 11

Upon Discovering a Close Friend or Relative with "Another" Man or Woman

A friend tells the story of the day he pulled up to a streetlight while driving in holiday traffic in town. He happened to glance into the car next to him and was shocked to see his brother-in-law sitting next to a beautiful blonde woman.

He had his arm around her. The woman was not the man's wife. Shocked at what he was seeing, my friend watched in disbelief as the brother-in-law kissed the woman passionately. When the light changed, the brother-in-law looked up to find my friend staring at him. Startled, my friend waved cheerily and drove on his way. The incident was never mentioned between the two. My friend was less concerned with the fact his wife's brother was having an affair, and being rather reckless about it at that, than he was with his own action. His question to me was, "Why did I wave?" It made him feel stupid. I agree that it did.

This is the twenty-first century folks, and people have affairs (not that this is a social characteristic of this century alone). We all know it. In some cases we have condoned it. In some cases, we have even participated. The question is, how do we handle the knowledge that someone close to us is having one?

In my friend's case, I think I was able to help. No. There is nothing I could really do about that wimpy wave. That is something with which he must live forever. However, I believe I was somewhat able to relieve his personal torment.

I must point out that it is my philosophy to seek an advantage in all things: to make a plus out of an apparent minus, to rise phoenix-like from the ashes of apparent failure. My advice, dear reader, will usually reflect this.

Now, to my friend.

The incident caused him great consternation. His wife was the cad's sister. His first dilemma was whether or not to tell his wife what he had seen. He demurred, largely because of his own ineffective response. Had he told her, he certainly would have been asked what his response had been. He would have found it more difficult to admit he had merely waved than to reveal her brother's transgression. So, fortunately, he did not tell his wife. I'll explain why it was fortunate in a moment.

He came to me some weeks later. He had lost weight, lost sleep, and lost a certain measure of self-respect by the time he got to me. I listened patiently and tried not to blanch too much when he described his reaction to the situation. As I have stated, however, I consider myself fairly proficient at making chicken salad out of horse poop.

His dilemma was not a dilemma at all, I explained. It was a gift from the Gods. He had been serendipitously empowered, I explained. He had achieved by accident what men and women, despots and kings, have sought to achieve through cunning over the ages. He now had total control over his brother-in-law.

There was no doubt that the brother-in-law had seen him, just as clearly as my friend had seen the ignoble man at that stoplight. The brother-in-law, therefore, knew that he had been spotted, and that my friend could, at any time he chose, blow the whistle and reveal the viper's vile behavior.

The fact that my friend never mentioned the incident to the man, and, in turn, the man never mentioned it to him, was, indeed, fortuitous. It enabled my friend to maintain that control.

The fact that he did not mention it to his wife was an equally happy accident. Had he mentioned it, his wife surely would have told her sister-in-law or confronted her brother. That would have created additional problems for my friend. Had the brother-in-law realized he had been ratted on, he would have forevermore sought revenge. And he would use any situation at his disposal to gain his vindictive end. Silence rendered all of this impossible, for the farthest thing from the brother-in-law's mind was, and always shall be, alienating *his* brother-in-law.

My friend even takes on heroic proportion in the cad's mind. Not having told gives him a status only men can appreciate, and increases the size of the debt the philanderer feels he must owe.

So, as I have explained to my buddy, that innocent wave was not the act of a wimp or a coward, as he first supposed, and as many might be expected to assume. No, it was a mailed fist being waved in the air. It was the trumpeting of the lead elephant in the herd. It was the call to arms of the hero who yells, "Follow me," while under fire.

Buoyed by my analysis, my friend further confessed that while he now feels better about his own role in the events I have described, he feels bad for his brother-in-law. The poor lout has lost forty pounds. Deep, dark circles have appeared under his eyes. He has been put on probation at work. He has been stricken recently with painful headaches and bursitis—all, apparently, while he waits for my friend to drop the proverbial shoe.

My pal told me he was beginning to feel guilty about not reassuring his brother-in-law that he would keep the secret. I simply reminded him that if he did that, his brother-in-law was likely, sooner or later, to make fun of him for having waved.

Chapter 12

How to Avoid a Fight

I'm afraid of getting beaten up!

One of my golden rules is to avoid violence at all costs. If this world is made up of lovers and warriors, I can say that I have frequently, though unsuccessfully, aspired to the former but have never been identified with the latter. If cowards truly die a thousand deaths while the valiant never taste of death but once, I have gone down multiple times and lived to cower another day. I work hard at avoiding confrontation.

Let's be clear. I'm not talking about walking down a dark alley and facing a thug, drunk, or a crackhead. I'm talking about spontaneous combustion, when rage comes out of nowhere and threatens bodily harm. It happens. Everyone seems to be going around with a chip on their shoulder these days.

To avoid possible altercations, it is advisable, even necessary, to develop strategies and tactics for dealing with aggression. A cool head and a keen eye help. So do props. I carry any number of them most of the time, including a bogus pair of glasses. They can be useful in many situations in which you are confronted by someone intent on inflicting pain. As I say, potential aggression is everywhere.

You cannot drive day after day without inadvertently cutting someone off, in return receiving lots of horn or a gesture in which the injured party is not using all of his or her fingers. The provocation need not be significant. Edging slightly out of one's lane. Stopping on yellow. Slipping into a parking spot seconds before someone else with obvious designs on the space. These transgressions, however innocent, can produce a nasty response.

That's just driving. The reaction is similar when you checkout at the supermarket express lane with twelve items rather than the requisite ten. Often nothing is said. However, you can count on a certain degree of animosity behind you in the line. It's often characterized by a nervous shifting of feet and/or mumbling in which you can decipher nothing more than a number (usually ten or twelve), or sense sounds that proclaim outright hostility.

There are occasions in restaurants or bars in which the lone male, who may or may not be on the prowl for a little companionship, may inadvertently let his gaze drift to a comely female. Holding the gaze can be dangerous if the female is accompanied by a male companion. Usually, in my experience, if the lady in question is alone, staring produces a quick turn of the head at best or a definitive "get lost" at worst. Every once in a while, it will reward the admirer with a sharp slap across the face.

I think you get the idea.

What must be avoided in any of the situations described, or any others in which there is any degree of real or perceived hostility, is to remain silent unless you have a carefully crafted strategy for dealing with angry confrontations. My defense mantra is that in a hostile situation anything that is said can be misconstrued or inflame. Even the most harmless comment can be interpreted as bellicose. That, almost assuredly, can lead to a physical threat or to someone actually making good on it.

We read in what's left of the daily paper of people being beaten to death, into unconsciousness, or "to within an inch of his life." Let's just assume that in all of these cases, broken bones and lacerations were an inevitable part of the process. It is crucial for each and every one of us who may harbor ill will, but with no proclivity to inflict harm or pain, to avoid running afoul of someone with opposite tendencies.

But how?

The easy answer is to avoid all such contact. But as I indicated at the outset, that is nigh impossible. One can't remove himself from society altogether. Most of us still have to drive to meet our daily responsibilities. If those responsibilities include shopping for staples at the local supermarket and you've miscounted, well, that can happen innocently. If eyes wander at a local watering hole, and they are mistakenly interpreted as provocative, suggestive, or intrusive, then a strategy must always be in place to counter any potential animosity.

The strategy is clearly designed to avoid situations that carry with them potential confrontation. If gestures, sighs, or averted gazes do not lead to immediate escalation, then you are home free. Most situations involving a degree of hostility do not go beyond annoyance to the aggrieved and represent nothing more than a nuisance. The affront will be forgotten by the time the injured party sits down at the dinner table—or in the case of the wandering eyes, perhaps the breakfast table.

I cannot take the time or space to cover every possible confrontation. However, let's take each example I cited earlier on, beginning with an infraction behind the wheel.

When I have finished you should get the idea and you can then quickly develop your own tactic for these and other situations. The strategy here is to be prepared at all times for a potential beating when hostility shows its ugly face. It will be up to you to develop the appropriate tactic on the spot. If you have no strategy, time will work against you with potentially painful consequences.

If someone displays animus when you are behind the wheel, you can hope that none of the cars stop. Then, there is no real chance for physical contact. However, remember to put a few cars between yourself and the aggrieved just to be on the safe side.

However, if you are without an escape route and forced for some reason to stop the car, there is a very simple way to calm the other driver. I favor carrying some sort of placard or flyer that will inspire a passive or friendly response. I carry an eight-by-ten piece of paper in my car and keep it easily accessible to the driver's seat. When the other driver gets out of his car and approaches with steam coming out of his ears, the situation can be defused by smiling and saying something like, "I'm glad you stopped. I'd like to show you this." At that point show him the paper, on which you had earlier written "Veterans for Peace." It helps to have that sign in red, white, and blue. You then tell the other driver that you are collecting for the organization and would welcome a donation. He will most likely do an abrupt about-face and return to his car. In some circumstances, he will actually give you a single, a five, or a ten and thank you for your service. I recommend having several of these "flyers" in case any driver takes the one you offered, and in case you have another incident the same day.

A variation on this strategy was used by a friend of mine in Texas. It was ill-advised. He preferred not to have to leave his car if he were stopped and faced a confrontation. He kept a small sign on the dash in front of his steering wheel. It read very simply: "Just Married." On the one or two occasions in which he had to show the sign, each of the potential aggressors smiled, waved in understanding, and returned to their cars. This works especially well if you are accompanied by a female. This tactic will not work as well if you are with a male companion, as my friend found out in what became a rather unpleasant escalation. The opposing driver took one look at the passenger, pulled out a gun, and shot out all four of my friend's car tires.

The solution at the supermarket express checkout is very simple and can be employed in any situation in which numbers are involved. If no one actually confronts you, you are in no danger. However, some of us who become aware of the animosity and want to move to put it in check, can do so rather effectively before some hothead attempts to throw you into the produce counter. Claim dyscalculia. It's a rare form of dyslexia and includes confusion about math symbols. And it's sometimes fun to do randomly just to watch the reaction of the cashier and to practice technique.

How to employ this tactic depends on whether someone confronts you before you actually get to the checkout clerk, or whether your sensory alert awakens as you are in the process of actually exchanging cash. For the former, challenge the accuser who undoubtedly is pointing to the sign announcing the limit on the number of items to check out. "What do you mean ten items?" you may say. "It clearly says twenty." The accuser's temperature will, by then, be on the rise. He may say, "Can't you read? It's ten!"

At the point of challenge you must slip into a different mode. "Oh no, it's happened again. I'm sorry, but I have occasional dyscalculia." That is usually met with a vacant stare. If you have followed my advice and carry bogus eyeglasses, this may be a good time to put them on. It helps to take them off quickly saying, "They don't help much." You can explain dyscalculia as you continue to move toward the cash register.

Generally, the volatility of the confrontation lessens, and you wind up retaining your place in line. When you are actually at the point of paying for your groceries, it is a nice touch to hand the checkout person two bills, say a five and a ten, and say, "Please take the appropriate bill. I have dyscalculia and can't read numbers." He or she will have never heard of the malady but will willingly assist you with your change, plus you may also receive a verbal or visual expression of sympathy as a bonus.

If the sensory alert comes as you are about to pay, and you have not had a conversation with restive shoppers to your rear, simply go ahead with the final portion of the above gambit and ask for help in selecting the currency in the proper denomination. Do so loudly so those behind you in line get the message. And, if you'd like to continue the ploy for their benefit, attempt to leave the store through the entrance door. It has nothing to do with dyscalculia, but can generate further sympathy. It's a nice touch that tends to corroborate your status as a somewhat confused person.

With apologies to those who are actually sick or disabled, I must confess a certain fondness, even partiality, to feigning some sort of physical disability to ward off an attack. I have been known to carry a cane in my car. It can be used as a weapon of sorts to help defend against outright aggression and/or as a prop to shame any would-be adversary. At a moment's notice I can walk with a pronounced limp even without the cane. Always available as a tactic is the outright fib, which, if handled effectively, can provide an escape hatch in most situations. Referring to a wife in labor at that moment can defuse a hostile situation. I must warn, however, that a thrashing is likely if the fib is revealed to be just that.

I should use this moment to differentiate between a fib and a lie. A fib is relatively benign in that while it is meant to deceive, it is generally intended to do so to save embarrassment to one party or the other—or, in our case, to avoid physical assault. The lie is an outright perversion of the truth. It is a deep-seated deception and is often malicious. I must admit, however, at times it also is used to avoid attack. I prefer the fib. And, if you are ever accused of lying and caught red-handed, admit only to a fib.

In the bar scenario, if a young lady who has been subject to your visual admiration and attention merely turns away, it's a no harm, no foul situation. However, if she is accompanied by a male companion, you may have to take action. (Notice I avoided using the term "swing" into action.) Sometimes taking the initiative can be useful.

I only recommend that approach if you detect signs that she is suggesting that her companion confront you, or if, at worst, he is showing signs he will use his weapons of mass destruction fists to punch your lights out.

If confronted by the woman or her companion, the simplest way to avoid fireworks is to offer an explanation that will work in any circumstance. If you have followed my advice and carry bogus eyeglasses, this may be a good time to put them on. Then you can say something like, "I didn't mean to stare. The young lady looks so much like a former classmate of mine. I was about to come over and ask if she went [and this is important] to the FBI Academy at Quantico in 1995 [choose any year that works]." Usually, the response is in the negative and the departure is accelerated, unless of course she did attend the academy. If so, I'm afraid you are on your own.

There are occasions when it is fairly obvious you are in for more than a complaint about ogling. It is usually preceded by an intense conversation between the woman and her companion, during which they turn frequently and fix their hostile gaze at you so that it's impossible to deny you are the subject of their discourse. This is where you have to take some initiative and make use of that creative limp I mentioned earlier. If you happen to have that cane normally stashed in your car, that can be helpful. Stand up and walk toward the couple, but do so slowly by limping awkwardly. The more pronounced the better. Quasimodo comes to mind as long as her name is not likely to be Esmeralda.

Upon arrival, apologize profusely and say, "I didn't mean to stare. The young lady looks so much like a former classmate of mine. I was about to come over and ask if she went to the FBI Academy at Quantico in 1995." You might continue, "I have lost track of my fellow agents since the shootout." Tapping the supposedly afflicted leg invariably creates a situation in which the couple in question is uncomfortable pursuing the conversation unless it is to express understanding and sympathy. Once again, the only possible variation of the scenario is if she did attend the academy. If so, as I mentioned, you are on your own.

The best course of action following your conversation with the couple is to leave the establishment. Don't forget the limp. If you remain, and you have to go to the men's room later, limp. If you do so in your natural gait, the consequences could be painful.

There are times when even the most carefully considered tactics will fail and you will find yourself in a position of imminent attack. When all else fails, drive away if you can, run away if you can, or . . . grovel and beg for forgiveness.

CHAPTER 13

When Something's Unsightly in a Partner's Nose

This is a tricky situation because it is embarrassing for you as well as for your partner. This situation occurs most often after blowing one's nose, or after a particularly hearty guffaw or laugh. It is possible for the remnant to go undetected by those hosting the offending practices for an entire evening, and, under the right circumstances, for days. I often use the blade of my knife as a mirror for an occasional dinner-table inspection. Unless a person happens to catch a reflection in a mirror, shiny plate, or piece of silverware, he or she can be totally unaware of this unsightly, usually sickening, freeloader.

One should always check one's nostrils when leaving the restroom. You can put your thumb and index finger to your nose from time to time to check, but this can become disconcerting to those around you. If you find something, problems can develop in getting rid of it without drawing attention, which is often difficult because people around you undoubtedly have been waiting for you to attend to the problem. As sickened or turned off as they may be while waiting, few will ever be forthright or considerate enough to reveal the source of their discomfort. However sad it is to say, you can never be quite certain something unsightly is there unless someone tells you.

As with much of my advice, I prefer to head off these problems before they happen. Because you don't want it to happen to you a lot more than you don't want it to happen to anyone else, even a loved one, the selfish approach is best.

First, tell your partner of your concern, and that you really hate it when you discover that something unsightly has been visible in your nose for several hours. Undoubtedly, he or she will admit a similar distaste. Work out a little signal. Tell your partner to tug his or her ear lobe if your nostril contains extra baggage.

This is a clear sign and very easy to read. You may certainly devise other signals or codes, and I encourage it. It can make for a nice game among understanding couples.

Once this is done, you can attend functions in relative security. I also advise you to remind your partner of the code from time to

time to ensure that he or she has not forgotten. One of my favorite techniques is to deliver an occasional signal and see how your mate or friend responds. You can usually tell by facial expression whether he or she has gotten the message. Fearing a problem, he or she will involuntarily put a finger near one or both nostrils. This can act as your confirmation that the code has been remembered.

Often, your partner will leave the room to attend to the situation. If the sign is missed, nothing will be done and there will be no change in facial expression. Yes, there is rarely any doubt whether the signal has been received or missed.

You have to be careful with these tests. If your partner catches on, he or she may send *you* an occasional false alarm. Thinking you have something hanging from your nose when you don't causes at least as much discomfort as thinking you have something hanging from your nose when you do.

If, under actual conditions, you send the signal and it is not responded to, it is not against the rules to say, "Do you remember our signal about tugging the ear lobe?" You may be surprised at the various expressions you can be faced with when your partner realizes what you are saying. Usually, you have to say nothing more. Still, try to get in sync without having to say anything. That way, there is no danger of being overheard, and you will not be subject to possible ridicule later from friends.

A friend of mine used to deal with the problem quite directly. I can recall one occasion in which his wife was sporting a particularly unattractive booger. At the dinner table, he simply said in a stage whisper, "You have something in your nose."

After getting over the shock, she fled the table, red-faced. Her cheeks were still quite crimson when she returned twenty minutes later. Her embarrassment, and his directness, could have been avoided by simply tugging an ear lobe.

One technique to avoid is cruel directness. Saying, "Get that thing out of your nose," or, "My God Mildred, you're making me sick," is a guaranteed way to invite a fight later. And, worse than that, your partner will await an opportunity to embarrass you to an even greater degree at a later date.

Chapter 14

Passing the Buck (or Blaming Others for Your Mistakes)

There are few techniques that are more time honored than passing the buck. We have all done it. Some, however, are able to do it with greater success than others. There is one cardinal rule that must never be violated when it comes to passing the buck: never ever do it in the presence of the person to whom the buck is being passed. It will earn you an enemy for life, and it will guarantee an act of retaliation.

Under ideal circumstances, the buck may be passed to someone who is deceased. This all but eliminates an opportunity for denial. It also greatly reduces the probability of a counter stroke.

When the occasion does present itself, simply say something like, "I warned John not to go for the project, but he was adamant." A nice touch in this situation, if events can support it, is to add, "I think he realized it just before he died." If the mistake was serious enough, it can lead to the impression that realizing the mistake contributed to John's death. In this case, you are off the hook. Check the newspaper obituaries daily.

Unfortunately, there is not always a fresh corpse to blame. As I often do, I advise thinking things out beforehand. Have a buck-passing plan. Let's face it, we all do it sooner or later. Why not have a plan?

The way to do that is to have a number of ready-made excuses at the tip of your tongue. If you can avoid blame when something goes wrong, shift blame, AND at the same time, get people to feel sorry for you, you have turned a potentially damaging situation into a plus.

These are the basic situations.

You are accused. "Did you know about this?" your boss might ask.

The implied accusation. "How could this have happened?" you may be asked. Clearly, the implication is that you know how it could have happened.

The befuddled statement. "How this might have happened is a mystery to me," is an admission that the person seeking information is in the dark. "We've got to get to the bottom of this," is a similar kind of admission.

Now, let's address these situations.

You must remember that the most important thing to do is to bring someone else's name into the equation as quickly as possible. You must deflect attention from yourself and put the "pass" back in passing the buck.

"Did you know about this?"

The preferred answer should be something like, "I should have realized what was going on when I heard *them* talking about it the other day."

You will be pressed as to who "them" might be. At this point say you heard the subject, whatever it might be, come up in the elevator or cafeteria at some earlier time. You paid no attention, you should be quick to explain, because you were engrossed in some project that you know to be one of the boss's priorities. The inquisitor will then be forced into a futile attempt to track "them" down.

"How could this have happened?"

Tricky, but try this. "I don't know, sir, this scenario never came up the other day when Jones and I were brainstorming this project." You might add, "Of course, I left early." If Jones is dead, you can go so far as to say, "I warned Jones about it just before he died."

The danger here is obvious. Jones, if he's alive, may well come to you after his own confrontation with the boss, and ask what the hell you were doing by bringing his name into it. Simply say the boss asked you the names of other people involved in the project, and that you gave him names but made no accusations. (I will explain later the value of the lie in the most critical situations. The lie can be one of life's most important tools, but I usually recommend it as a remedy only for the most unpleasant situations.)

"We've got to get to the bottom of this," gives you your out.

Clearly, the befuddled spokesperson has no clue as to what went wrong. The key to this scenario is obviously the contraction "we've." Seize the opportunity. Say, "Yes, WE do, and I'll work with you day and night until we know what for." Offer to work closely with the other person. This reinforces your loyalty, dedication, and willingness to take on extra work. It also puts you in the middle of the investigation so you can protect yourself.

There are other techniques. When confronted, proclaim that you left a message warning of the predicament on the boss's answering machine, voice mail, or e-mail. Few people will question the possibility of this technology's failure. When pressed, confess (only if you have to) that you might have left the message at someone else's number. It's helpful to know the boss's number, and say something like, "I know I dialed 5-7-6." When he says, "My number is 5-6-7," you simply respond, "Yes, I know. Isn't that what I said?" It will confuse him and further implant the probability that you misdialed. Usually, it will set him on another tack.

You can often blame things on the slowness of the U.S. Mail, a courier service, a faulty phone system, or one of a variety of viruses on the Internet.

Another proven winner is to blame your wife. If you received any messages related to the tainted project at home, simply say your wife never told you. It's even better to blame it on a child.

I have a friend who actually fabricated the birth of a child so he might have myriad excuses for many things in his professional career. He often got a little time off by claiming his child was sick. He had a built-in excuse when he was late by claiming he had to leave the child at day care. Of course, he often left work early claiming he had to retrieve the child. At one time, sensing that he might be caught in corporate downsizing, he told everyone who would listen that his child was afflicted with a life-threatening disease. It was a highly effective ploy.

CHAPTER 15

Upon Receiving Incorrect Change

This is the one that shows us of what we are made. There is no internal debate when we have received too little change. We simply point it out, take what is owed us, and accept the cashier's apology. No, the demons appear when we have received too much change, and we are faced with the dilemma of accepting it or returning it.

The debate is simple. It's the decision that's tough. We all know that it is basically dishonest to knowingly take more than what we are due. We all know that ultimately the person who made the mistake will pay for it. It is commonplace for tellers, cashiers, and clerks to make up the difference when there's a discrepancy at the end of the day. They are not allowed to keep any overage. However, when they are short, it usually comes out of their own pockets.

We, however, do not suffer the burden of the clerk's credo that "the customer is always right."

When we point out a shortage in our change, the clerk is honor bound to make up the difference. In fact, I have seen clerks and cashiers make up the shortfall when I have been certain they did not believe the customer.

So when we notice that some unwitting clerk has shoved two twenty-dollar bills into our hand instead to two fives or two tens, there is an adrenal rush, a surge of heat, a flush, a quickened heartbeat, and the unique satisfaction of knowing that we have gotten that which is so elusive: we have gotten something for nothing. The feeling is enhanced by the realization that there is something basically dishonest about taking it and saying nothing. It is the microcosm of the perfect crime.

There is beauty in the innocence of it. You may accept the money and put it in your pocket or purse. Even if the clerk should realize his or her mistake, you can feign innocence by insisting that you had not noticed. You can respond with any one of several approaches, or a combination thereof.

You can return the overage, make a joke, and kick yourself all the way home for its having been noticed before you were able to make a safe getaway.

My personal favorite is to react as offended, as if wrongly accused of a crime. What's nice about this technique is the pain is not quite as bad as it is when you kick yourself all the way home. AND there is the off chance that the clerk, afraid of having violated that "tie goes to the customer" credo, will acquiesce and allow you to continue with no further challenge.

You also (and this takes some chutzpah) can simply glance in your purse or billfold and deny the overage—then casually stroll out of the store. This technique can backfire. I have heard of situations in which store detectives get into the act and cause an embarrassing scene at the door of the shop.

If this should happen to you, don't panic. They may ask to see your purse or billfold. They may even ask you to tell them how much money you are carrying (as if any of us ever really knows), and they may try to intimidate you in other ways. Stick to your guns. They have no way of proving that any money in your possession belongs to them, unless you have just robbed a bank and the red dye charge has gone off. That's an entirely different story.

Chapter 16

How to Keep Friends from Using Your Pool

Anyone who has ever owned a swimming pool knows the problem. People you know well, people you know slightly, and people you don't know at all are constantly fishing for invitations.

I have a friend whom I see occasionally. However, during the summer months, he will always ask, "How's your pool?" It is as transparent as an algae-free, twenty-by-forty-foot kidney-shaped.

The problem is that during the first year we had the pool I was always telling friends to come on over any time. Many took me up on it and continued to do so the next year, and the next, and the next, until I figured out how to deal with it.

Maintaining a pool is difficult and expensive enough as it is. However, keeping a handy supply of liquor, beer, soda, hot dogs, hamburgers, ribs, and assorted snacks on hand for the drop-in crowd is expensive. It also takes up a lot of space.

Also, after a long hard day or week at the office, my wife and I do treasure a little time to ourselves. Our teenage kids are no problem. They don't swim at our pool. They go to someone else's. Clearly, when you have a pool, spending time alone is difficult. The solution came to me in the form of a problem.

A couple of years ago, I came home from work on a hot July night, wanting nothing more than a can of Bud and a swim. The thought of it had sustained me through the day. When I got home, I saw the pool water sparkling as I pulled into the garage. I remember it striking me as a little odd that no one was in the water. All the better, I thought.

I was inside in a bound and quickly into my suit. Seconds later, I was on the patio, struck by the sight of my wife taking a long slug from a Martini. She looked pasty under her tan.

"What's the matter?" I asked.

"Jeremy threw up in the pool," she answered. Jeremy is a neighborhood six-year-old, whom I had come to hate. He was loud and spoiled rotten. He never asked to be invited, and this particular summer he had taken to wandering into our house whether we wanted him to or not. We never did. He helped himself to the video games and had no problem at all taking anything he wanted from the refrigerator.

I didn't much care for his parents either. They showed up around 4:00 p.m. most Saturdays. Once, they didn't leave, even when my wife and I went to a wedding. I still think they invited friends over when we were gone.

Horrified at my wife's words, I wandered to the edge of the pool. Sure enough, there was gastronomical detritus everywhere. Bits and pieces of it floated on the surface. A disturbingly large amount rested on the bottom. It looked like the kid had been eating strawberries, hamburgers, pickles, French fries, along with other less identifiable matter.

My desire to swim vanished. I felt slightly sick to my stomach myself. I went inside and made a martini of my own, putting it in an oversized coffee cup.

My wife and I sat speechless for half an hour. I finally waddled to the pool. My stomach started to churn once more. I skimmed and vacuumed for the better part of an hour, retrieving all the offensive matter I could. Some remained on the bottom, impervious to my efforts. I was hopeful it would disintegrate overnight. It did not. Not all of it. Much of the residue was still visible the next morning.

To make a long story short, it was a week before I or my wife could make ourselves get into that pool. Kids and neighbors came and went as usual, swimming with ignorance of what had happened. Oddly, neither Jeremy nor his parents showed up for ten days or so.

It came to me in a flash one night; triumph seized from adversity. If my wife and I would not swim in our own pool because a snotty kid had thrown up in it, and if the kid himself and his parents were prolonged no-shows, would anyone else swim in our pool if I told them I had gotten sick in it? It was worth a try.

The next day was Saturday. I was up early in the morning and off to the novelty store in the mall. I bought several packages of fake vomit and put it all in the pool as soon as I got home. Then I waited for the kids, some of whom would be accompanied by parents, to show up. Shortly after noon, they did.

I made sure I was poolside. "Kids," I said, "I don't think you'll want to swim until I clean the pool." I watched with glee as they digested (not a great choice of words) what was in the pool. "I don't know what came over me," I said. "I must be getting the flu or something."

I needed to say nothing more. Within ninety seconds, all were gone. Only one or two ventured back during the rest of the summer.

There were times in later seasons when I had to resort to other, but no-less-effective methods. One day we had half a dozen three- to six-year-olds splashing around with their parents. I managed to slip a Baby Ruth candy bar—à la *Caddyshack*—into the deep end when no one was watching. It was spotted by one of the mothers a few minutes later. Everyone was out of the pool quickly. It was actually quite humorous to watch the little ones look at their friends accusingly.

Within ten minutes, all parents and kids were gone, as if by magic.

I have another trick up my sleeve in case the uninvited visits continue. It is amazing how my techniques have cut the crowds. Nonetheless, each year, the season still begins with a wave of unexpected, unannounced visitors. Next year, I plan to put green dye into the pool the day it's opened. I'll make it look like a primordial pond and explain that the discoloration was caused by some mysterious rash-causing algae that chemists were still pondering. That ought to hold them for the season. But I'll still keep a few Baby Ruths around, just in case.

CHAPTER 17

The Toilet Seat

My research shows that only money ranks as a greater source of friction between husbands and wives than the raised toilet seat. There are women who actually have vowed to kill their mates because of their failure to lower the toilet seat after use.

There are men who have vowed to kill their spouses because of panty hose draped over the shower curtain, or because of assorted creams, jellies, and salves crammed into the bathroom medicine cabinet. For my money, men have the more convincing argument. My wife thinks otherwise. Stalemate! I continue to leave the toilet seat up. But getting into the shower for me is like maneuvering in a synthetic nylon triple-canopy jungle. However, our truce does not end the broader debate.

The problem, of course, is that men traditionally leave the seat up after using the facility. Inattentive women, entering the W.C., intent on their own mission, have been known from time to time to sit on the toilet before returning the seat to the "sitting" position. The result is usually a wet discomfort, accompanied more often than not by a very unladylike comment, and, sometimes, even a little pain. I should note here that no women of my acquaintance have ever been seriously injured in this fashion. In fact, the greatest harm seems to come to small children hearing a part of their mother's vocabulary that would be better kept from them.

Resulting arguments between parents may do some psychological harm to the youngsters. It is difficult to calculate that. Any damage done to young psyches in this manner is unfortunate. I think it would be a mistake, however, to dwell too heavily on residual damage to offspring resulting from the general failure of men to put down the toilet seat.

Our effort here is not to assess blame. It is to address the problem and provide solutions. Solutions are what matter, not tradition and not social pressure administered from parties not *privy* to the problem. Political correctness is not a factor in our attempt to help people.

This debate has been going on for a long, long time. Better minds than mine have attempted to deal with it. Let's concede that men, in general, are not likely to begin putting down the toilet seat any more quickly than a woman is likely to be ready to leave for a party on time.

As I see it, there are several ways to approach the problem. First, let's take the fairest approach. Men and women should simply consider it a draw. The panty hose vs. the toilet seat evens everything out. Two wrongs don't make a right. While that is generally true, I think this situation may be an exception.

However, if this is unacceptable to the affected parties, there are other approaches. One employed by a friend of mine is ingenious, if perhaps a little overdone. He has attached a chime to the light in the bathroom. Every time the light is turned on, the first notes of Beethoven's Fifth ring out. The problem with this reminder is that the toilet seat dilemma generally rears its ugly head at night. Women get up from bed and tiptoe into the bathroom, wishing not to disturb anyone else sleeping in the house. It is for this reason that they often don't turn on the lights at all and therefore never see the raised seat. The musical reminder becomes a liability in these circumstances. Women would be even less likely to turn on the light so as to protect the rest of the household from the noise. So, I do not recommend this method. It is counterproductive.

Another suggestion is to tie a large red (color optional) bow to the seat until all parties become sufficiently used to toilet seat protocol. It is merely habit after all. The problem with this method, needless to say, is that the bow can tend to get in the way when the seat is in place and ready for use. Some jokesters have even suggested that the bow be tied elsewhere—on the man himself perhaps. Most men blanch at this prospect, though one did once recommend a tattoo.

Separate bathrooms has been suggested. That, however, is only for the rich.

There are some who suggest removing the seat altogether, and letting people get used to that. This option is usually offered by men and quickly rejected by women. Others ask why men are required to put the toilet seat down when women are not admonished to raise it when they've finished?

Divorce has been proffered, and in some cases accepted as a solution.

There are those who have proposed putting a big note on the wall just in front of the toilet. That can disrupt the decor.

Others recommend putting a big, tasteful picture, in keeping with the decor, over the porcelain. It is my thought that time would diminish recollection of why it's there.

There are any number of devices that can be employed as reminders. All have merit to a greater or lesser degree.

As I mentioned, it is a thorny problem with no simple answer. However, a very practical solution may be the simplest. Men, just use the bathroom sink, and, for a little variety, the shower. No one will ever know, and you will forever be a hero in your own home. The beauty of this solution is that you can nag at your wife over those damn pantyhose whenever you like. Her rejoinders will be limited.

Chapter 18

Upon Inviting All Your Kindergartner's Friends to a Party, and then Realizing You Left Out the Class Brat

Many parents will recognize this dilemma. Your precious little kindergartner, Irmgard or Sven, wants a birthday party and is anxious to invite his or her classmates. It is a large group of twenty or so children. The burden of hosting such a bash is considerable and should be accepted only after a great deal of thought. I personally prefer to limit the number of children to parties for kids under the age of sixteen to two or, at the most, three. Nonetheless, some parents feel they are up to a larger number. More power to them.

There are inherent dangers. With a group of twenty, there is a good chance that one of them will get sick and soil your carpet or furniture. There is also a chance one of the little buggers will be harboring germs of one sort or another, all but guaranteeing that your own child, and perhaps even you, will come down with any one of a variety of unpleasant illnesses in subsequent days.

You can count on something of value getting broken. At least one of the little communists will cry during the party. And, horror of horrors, with a batch of five- and six-year-olds on hand, at least one and perhaps more will wet his or her pants.

Another negative is the certainty that one child will be picked up late. Sometimes, it can be an hour or two late. This is infuriating. It is indescribably unfair of the tardy parent. However, it will happen. I've known parents who use a child's birthday party as a babysitting opportunity and go shopping or even out to dinner while their little one is being entertained. Courts have been known to be understanding in cases where the hostess has threatened or performed physical harm to the tardy parent.

Generally, the host or hostess is exhausted by the time the party is over. (By the way, the attending parent is almost always the wife. Husbands have long since learned how to avoid such occasions. See my postscript.) I prefer to greet the dilatory parent in the following manner. Simply say, out of the child's earshot, that the little one seems to be okay *now*. You will note a look of alarm. Hasten to add that the Heimlich Maneuver worked to perfection and that the little brat had hardly even gotten red before the birthday candle was dislodged from its throat. The mother will undoubtedly question the child about the incident later. The youngster, of course, will deny the occurrence, likely provoking an argument on the trip home. It may even begin the erosion of trust between child and parent.

While there is considerable opportunity for unpleasantness at these events, one opportunity presents special problems. There is clearly a moment of panic just before the party, or sometimes just after it has started, when you realize that one of your child's classmates was not invited. Some won't show because of a conflict in commitments, sickness, or whatever. But in every case I can recall, one child is always singled out for premeditated exclusion. Part of the problem is that you know the missing youngster will learn of the party from thoughtless, even taunting, classmates. Let's face it, if the kid wasn't invited, he's already unpopular.

It is a parent's nightmare to think that they have been party to what amounts to the blackballing of one youngster. The panic also stems from the realization of what both the parent and child would feel if they had been similarly snubbed. Kids do not take it well, although there is a body of evidence suggesting they tend to react somewhat better than adults to having been slighted. Parents will worry that they will be retaliated against at some point in time. I have known parents waiting for that particular shoe to fall throughout their child's entire school career. It is not pleasant.

If the hosting parent learns of the exclusion in time, there is always a chance of making it good and getting out the invitation. You can claim the party was an impromptu idea. However, you run the risk of humiliating the youngster once he or she arrives. Chances are the kid will be ostracized at the party itself. And, usually, this is the child who throws up or wets his or her pants, or worse. The pure and simple fact of the matter is that if your child did not want that particular youngster at the party, there is generally a pretty good reason. Kids aren't dumb. The missing kid is probably a brat.

Life being what it is, you probably won't learn of the rebuff until just before the party starts, during the party, or even afterward. Obviously, short of calling the absent child's parents and the youngster himself or herself and apologizing later, there is nothing that can be done about it. Such a call, in any case, is difficult and requires an imaginative lie.

One way to handle it is to call and inquire as to why the little tyke was unable to make the party. Ask if he or she is all right. Thinking they have misplaced an invitation, or that their child forgot to mention the party to them, this puts the other parent on the defensive. In turn, it gives you a hefty social advantage, and there is a bonus in that it frequently leads to an additional present for your child.

POSTSCRIPT

Husbands who want to bail out of the type of party I have just described should not worry. Normally, this would be worth a segment unto itself. However, it has been my observation that most, if not all, fathers already have mastered the technique of avoiding such events. It is an honored ability and probably genetic.

Chapter 19

Forgetting Someone's Name

This is truly an embarrassing situation and one we have all experienced. I believe it has to do with context. We might meet people under one set of conditions, then run into them in an entirely different situation. For instance, after a round of golf, your partner may introduce you to his doctor while you are all showering. You rinse soap off your hands, shake hands, make a little small talk, and go your separate ways.

Two weeks later, while attending a fund-raiser, a fully clothed doctor approaches you, extends his hand, and says, "Nice to see you again." It is one of life's moments of truth.

Chances are you have no clear recollection of the man. You may know that you've met him someplace. Five will get you ten that you can't remember where you met, much less his name. An interesting byproduct is the probability of putting your new friend at a disadvantage. He has probably forgotten your name and where you met as well. There is no feeling quite as satisfying as knowing you have one-upped someone, especially a perfect stranger who is showing disturbing signs of wanting to be a friend. Establish superiority in the relationship at the outset, and you will maintain it forever.

You have to think fast. Your wits must be about you at all times in any social situation. When you are called to draw my advice into practice, there is never time to reflect. Your response must be instantaneous and automatic if you wish to avoid embarrassment. I suggest practice, practice, and more practice.

You might try it in the car, preferably when you're alone. You can also do it in the shower, or while walking the dog.

Here's how it works. You are in the middle of the room during a cocktail party. You can see the advance from the corner of your eye. You sort of recognize a distinguished gentleman on the other side of the room. Your eyes meet, and you see a flicker of recognition in his. He begins to make his way toward you. You know you've met but have no recollection of where, much less his name.

It is imperative that you begin your strategy the moment he begins to move in your direction.

First, smile broadly. You must give the impression you are happy to see him again. It will disarm him.

Then, the conversation should go very much like this.

"Hello," you say, beaming. "Nice to see you again."

"Same here," he says. If he's good he'll also be smiling broadly.

Now, here is where it takes guts.

"I've thought of you often since we last met," you say.

"Thank you," he'll likely respond. "I have thought of you also." This is probably a lie.

Now, for the quick kill. "You know, my father and you share the same name," you say. At this point, it is okay to relax the smile a bit as if fondly remembering your dear old dad.

"His name is Ellis, also?" is the response. Bingo. You are home free. Unless your last name is Ellis, he will have given you his first name. You have to have nerves of steel for this game. Nonetheless, you can refer to him for the entire evening as "My friend, Ellis." The introduction applies equally well for first or last names.

If he truly does not know your name, and this is likely, he will be uneasy wondering whether your last name is Ellis. It will likely hasten his departure.

The best person I ever saw at this technique was a fortyish woman with the nerves of a combat pilot. I think she was in real estate. She was clearly in command when she met an anonymous acquaintance at a party. I overheard the following conversation.

"How lovely to see you again." Her voice dripped with sincerity.

"You are looking lovely, as usual," came the response. They were both very good actually.

"I think of you often," my friend said. "Do you know you share the same name as my mother?" She gave it a nice touch. "I think you spell it differently."

"Does she spell it E-D-N-A," came the woman's reply, not knowing she had been hooked.

This is where full concentration is a must. "See," my friend chirped. "She spelled it A-E-D-N-A."

The spelling ploy can be ingenious. Work with names in your spare time.

"He spelled it J-O-H-N."

"Dad spelled it J-O-N."

Take any name; Dorothy, Mary, Peter, Roy, and they can become Dorothea, Mare, Petre, and Roye. However, you must be very quick to play this game. You can usually add an "e" or an "a" somewhere and make it work for you. Doubling vowels is a nice trick too.

CHAPTER 20

Changing Subjects When You Have No Interest in What Someone Is Saying, or Don't Understand What They're Talking About

We have all met people who bore us. Sometimes, it's because we are not interested in what they like to talk about. Sometimes, it's because we don't understand what they are talking about. It makes no difference, really. When confronted by these people, our eyes have a tendency to glaze, our blood pressure rises, our anxiety level increases, and we think to ourselves, "How do we get out of here?"

But it doesn't work that way, because if we could simply leave, we would. We could employ almost any ploy. "I've got to catch a train." Or, "My house is on fire." You get the idea. A quick excuse is always appropriate, whether it's the truth or not. *Excuse* means to justify or to release from obligation. My dictionary makes no mention of the word *truth*.

However, the sad fact is that entrapment by boredom is all too often the work of someone for whom a simple fabrication is not enough. It can be an in-law, a minister, a boss, a teacher. In short, someone from whom we just can't apologize and run. We have to stand tall and face the music, unless we can find a way to end the tedium that does not discredit, and will satisfy, your companion.

There are several dangers here. If you do not respond at all, you will offend. If you feign interest and ask a question or two, you are likely to (1) prolong the one-sided conversation, or (2) show you have not been paying attention by asking a foolish question. There is no quicker giveaway of one's inattentiveness than to politely ask a question and have the answer begin, "As I just said . . ."

Let's set the following scenario. Your minister comes to call and launches quickly into a soliloquy about the Old and New Testaments. You are expert in neither and fear a question that will show your ignorance.

(This is not part of this segment, but when you sense a question you don't wish to answer, quickly ask one of your own. It is

a violation of the strategy against prolonging a conversation, but it will save you some embarrassment. In this case I suggest, "How does each relate to the Koran?" Then sit back and try to relax. It is likely to be a long afternoon. If you don't care about the embarrassment, then by all means, don't ask a question.)

One technique for ending the conversation is to suggest that the two of you go for a walk to enjoy God's bounty. You should be fairly certain, however, that the minister (1) does not have time for a walk, (2) suffers from some discomfort or disability that might preclude the possibility, or (3) has allergies. If you are fortunate enough to be visited during a rain or snow storm, suggest the walk anyway. It usually causes a shift in the subject being discussed. And therein lies the secret of this strategy.

Say your boss comes to call and is regaling you with the merits of your rival or with the invoicing system currently being used so successfully in the Honduras office. Perhaps he attempts to convince you that his hobby is just right for you.

You may be trapped by your child's physics teacher, who takes it upon him or herself to explain to you the theory of relativity.

An in-law may take it upon him or herself to describe the last vacation in intricate detail, complete with slides and video. These are but a few of the possibilities. They are literally endless.

However, my method of dealing with these situations works very nicely. It comes from an old Dale Carnegie suggestion. It is this: Shift the topic of conversation to yourself at all costs. This is the only effective way to deal with the problem.

The late Mr. Carnegie wrote that if you wish to make someone feel he or she has had a good conversation with you, either talk about them or let them talk about what they want to talk about. My technique turns that 180 degrees. If people enjoy talking to you about themselves or the things that interest them, it follows that they will not enjoy it if you force the conversation into a discussion of you and your interests. It should bring the entire conversation to a rather abrupt conclusion. It has the additional advantage that you are likely to be so boring they will never again seek to become engaged in an extended conversation with you.

Take the case of our minister. If he insists on discussing the various translations of the Bible, you might suggest something like, "I wish there were a section on plumbing in the Bible. I could use the Lord's help in our upstairs bathroom. Come on up, I'll show you. I'd better forewarn you though. The toilet hasn't been flushed in a week." You'll probably be getting the reverend his hat at the bottom of the stairs rather than subject him to plumbing talk.

As to the boss, well, I have never met a boss who wanted to look as if he didn't know everything. He may have been advised on the efficiency of the Honduran invoicing system, but chances are he doesn't really understand it. You can press him for the most insignificant details. Or take advantage of my choice and use the opportunity to tell him how you decided to make a career in his field. If he presses on with a discussion of his passion, stamp collecting, tell him every post office horror story you have ever heard. You can talk about long waits, discourtesy, or, if you like, suggest some theories of your own as to why fired postal workers so often seek revenge by blowing away colleagues.

As to the teacher, at the first opportunity, make reference to his world, and yours. Something like, "There is the physical world . . . and there is the fiscal world. Right now, I'm taking a beating in my mutual funds." A sentence or two about stock market fluctuations and ideas you might have for investing HIS money usually makes quick work of the situation. In fact, if you can steer the conversation to the notion of extracting money from the other person, the conversation will end rapidly. Asking how much he makes is a good ploy.

Ask the minister if the church has a loan fund.

Ask the boss for more money to implement a new system in your department. Or ask if he'd like to subscribe to the monthly newsletter you put out on your favorite subject, derivative stock speculation. (If he says "yes," find another job.)

Ask the relative to lend you several thousand dollars for YOUR next vacation.

In all of these scenarios, one of two things will happen. Any and all might actually comply with the request for a loan or more money for the job. Or, more likely, they will find a reason for a quick exit. In either case you come out ahead.

CHAPTER 21

How to Get Around Forgetting an Anniversary, Birthday, or Some Other Important Occasion

Very few of us have managed to avoid forgetting an important occasion at one time or another. There is no painless way to come out of it. Forgetting an anniversary can be cause for such anxiety as to give the offending party cramps, seizures, and headaches of a magnitude never dreamed of by Mr. Richter. In some cases, the pain is psychologically produced. Often, it also is produced externally, most often by the offended party.

In all fairness, this forgetfulness problem is suffered more by men than by women. There is no rational way to explain this. My own estimate is that men are responsible for 98.73 percent of all memory lapses related to birthdays and special occasions. The remainder are forgotten by women and children, but this is usually the result of a personal trauma, such as a death in the family, a job loss, moving, kidnapping, or divorce. Research also shows that divorce has produced an entirely new category for the subject. That, of course, is forgetting a birthday or anniversary on purpose.

Exacerbating the problem of memory lapse is the fact that women generally leave no time to counter or recover. They have been known to wait until midnight on the anniversary or birth date before mentioning it. The human ego is such that women generally believe that you are waiting until the last possible moment to "surprise" them. The problem with this assumption is that when the reminder does not come until midnight, it is too late to do anything about it. In time, that is. And timing is everything in these circumstances.

An anniversary or birthday gift that comes a day late is no better than no gift at all. Some women will not mention a forgotten occasion for several days. They are not giving the husband or boyfriend a grace period. Such women are just inherently cruel. If days pass before you realize your omission, all is lost. This is most likely to occur after fifteen or twenty years of marriage.

Conversely, the bride will often awake on the date in question and say something like, "Isn't this a wonderful day for an anniversary [or birthday]," giving the spouse the opportunity to hint broadly that the best is yet to come. He then has the entire day to make up for his lapse and recover. Her naivety is generally short lived. Women, I have observed, prefer the "test and guilt" method. No hints. They like to be reassured that the big occasion did not need a reminder. And, if the test is failed, a generous heaping of guilt will be ladled on the hapless spouse.

Frankly, I don't know what they did in days before Sunday sales became acceptable. Once every seven years or so, every man was susceptible to a Sunday memory lapse with no ability to recover until Monday because stores were closed. This used to be called "the seven year twitch." Since Blue Laws have been repealed in most states, it is now referred to as the "seven year itch" and means something quite different indeed.

As I mentioned earlier, there is no painless way out of this memory morass. On some occasions, if one is skillful, he can use pain to his advantage. During the course of the day in question, there are often signs that something is amiss. The wife will often refuse to speak to her mate. It is obvious from her first waking moment if she senses he has forgotten the occasion. No extra sensory perception needed here. If he wakens and does not make mention of the day's significance immediately, she'll know.

Once she does, if she speaks at all, it is often with sarcasm. This treatment will likely continue all day and reach the apogee at

dinnertime. (She, of course, had fully expected to be taken out to dinner.) After a day of waiting, the frustration and growing anger usually result in the woman making the man's least favorite meal, then literally shoving his plate at him. I warn all men to be aware of these signs. When they first appear, feign a migraine headache. Claim severe stomach cramps if need be. Do anything to appear to be in great physical discomfort. It is a recommended course of action for any unexplained hostility.

The ancient Chinese realized that the mind does not work as it should when one is in considerable physical distress. Although the Chinese have been researching the connection between pain and forgetfulness for centuries, women have experimented over a longer period of time.

The work of the Chinese, by the way, came in connection, not with forgetting, but with remembering. Since time immemorial, the Chinese have experimented with using pain to help revive one's memory. It was only one quick step from that research that brought them to the other studies.

One hundred percent of American women, a Chinese friend told me, accept the notion that there is, and should be, a direct connection between pain and forgetting. Therefore, let me remind you that the instant you become aware of the above-mentioned characteristics in your spouse, you would do well to conclude instantly that they are a classic, early stage indication that you have forgotten an important occasion. You immediately should seek to determine the exact nature of the oversight and correct it. Time can be critical.

If you are lucky, or newly married, not to suggest that the two are mutually exclusive, the pain ploy might work. More often than not, however, it will not.

Another pitfall of forgetting an important occasion is that only the most sadistic of women will present your gift before she has received her own. When she does, it is usually near that midnight deadline, and she usually does it either to inspire your presentation or watch your own suffering and discomfort as you realize, as she has, that you have forgotten and that there is no opportunity to counter. On the day in question, however, most women will present nothing, say nothing, and otherwise offer no hints or clues as to the nature of their foul mood.

Men, you are therefore, for all practical purposes, out there on your own left with nothing more than your own cleverness in dealing with the dilemma. That word, *dilemma*, is perhaps too benign. Crisis, is more like what you are faced with, and it should be dealt with accordingly.

As I have suggested earlier, once the unwitting sap of a husband is ensnared in this difficult web of deception, anger, humiliation, and malice that has been brought on by a single episode of forgetfulness, there is no way to proceed without pain. Pain is inflicted for forgetting in the first place. That does not end it. It is inflicted throughout the entire period, up to and including recovery, and beyond!

Frequently, to compensate, men have spent enormous amounts of money on gifts of absolution. For after having forgotten an anniversary, birthday, or other special occasion, your gift is no longer a gift for the occasion. It is seeking . . . no . . . begging, forgiveness. Some women forgive. Remember, however, that none ever forget. Ever!

It has led to physical pain, psychological pain, and, as I indicated earlier, even divorce. There have been a few documented cases of homicide. More than a few men have been cuckolded as a result of a single lapse. It is not pretty. There is virtually no recovery. No matter how the hand is played, ultimately there is some form of punishment.

Now, to dealing with it. There is only one way. Buy the gifts now. Right now! This moment. Don't delay. Don't give yourself a chance to forget. Inasmuch as this is the characteristic that causes the problem in the first place, this may be the most important advice.

Buy a gift, or two, and several cards. I suggest an anniversary card, a birthday card, or generic cards on which an inscription fitting any occasion can be noted.

Purchase nice gifts. Jewelry usually is best. Wrap them in paper suitable for all occasions. A nice heavy white paper works very well.

Then, hide the gifts carefully. This is very important. If you are careless about it, and your woman finds these gifts, she will immediately and automatically conclude that you are unfaithful. This produces pain of another kind. It compares unfavorably to the misery experienced when one forgets an important occasion.

Always keep the gifts in the house. They will do you no good at all if they are in the office or at your summer place. If you have a summer place, however, you might stash at least one gift there, just in case.

Some men keep the gifts in the car. The tool bag is a favorite spot. I do not recommend using the car for this purpose. Imagine the consequences if your car were stolen on or around the anniversary or birthday. Or if it were undergoing repairs in a garage. After being victimized or having an automobile breakdown, the chances are greater than ever that you will forget the imminent special occasion. That just makes a bad situation worse. A lot worse!

Also, when confronted at that midnight deadline, you do not win many points for yourself if you admit you have left the precious gift in the car, especially if she sees you fishing around for it in a tool bag. Furthermore, if your wife should happen to accidentally find the articles in your vehicle, you forever will be suspected of infidelity.

I recommend placing the gifts in your golf bag. This may require your taking up the game.

I have known men who have resisted stashing gifts. Believe me, they like to live dangerously. "It can't happen to me," they have been known to say, only to suffer a variety of consequences later. The cold hard truth is that it can happen to you, and probably will sooner or later. I can only advise you how to be ready and why.

Let me add this postscript.

There are ways in which you can skillfully remind a loved one that an important date is approaching. This can save everyone a lot of misery. To wives, who need no reminding, but who want to be sure the spouse does not forget an important date, I suggest putting a large calendar in the kitchen. At the beginning of the year, circle the important dates in red. Make it a bold mark that no one can miss. This is a nice tactic if you have children. Thinking it means something for them, they will usually ask the significance of the mark. This usually generates some discussion around the household.

To men, I suggest they buy a notebook calendar of their own every year or invest in a computer calendar program with a "reminder" function. They should take a moment or two and note the important dates, if they can remember them, and cite the specific occasion. When you see a date circled in red on your wife's calendar, retrieve your own hard copy or digital source and determine the special occasion.

Finally, men, if you are fortunate enough to have a secretary, make full use of that employee. Instruct him or her to give you two days' notice of all important dates and that failure to do so can result in instant termination. However, don't rely solely on this method. If the secretary fails, or is off sick, your wife will never blame the secretary. She will blame you.

To men, if you are clever, and you have not forgotten the occasion, there is nothing wrong with you waking and saying to your wife or girlfriend, "My, isn't this a nice day for an anniversary [or birthday]." It creates quite the opposite of all the misery I have alluded to above.

Finally, women, there is nothing wrong with you waking on

the day in question and saying something like, "My, isn't this a beautiful day for an anniversary [or birthday]." It is a guarantee that the occasion will not be forgotten and will give a grateful man plenty of time during the day to find you a nice present suitable for the occasion. And, if you are clever, you can probably do it four or five times a year.

Chapter 22

When Someone Asks You to Guess His or Her Age

This can be very tricky and requires an absolute ability to fib with alacrity. There are some very basic rules to remember, and woe be the one who confuses these rules.

You must remember that women like to be told they seem younger.

Men like to be told they are in terrific shape for their age (always guess low).

Old people like to tell you their age, so generally no guessing is involved. You must follow by telling them they look like they have the energy and vigor of someone years younger.

Boys up to age eighteen or nineteen like to be told they look older than they are (this is generally so they can feel they can buy beer without being detected).

Girls up to age eighteen like to be told they look up to four or five years older. After age twenty-one, they must always be told they look younger.

So, there is no trick to it. Compliments, graciousness, diplomacy. No problem. However, this chapter is titled what to do "When Someone Asks You to *Guess* His or Her Age." This puts a whole new wrinkle on the problem.

To begin with, it is inherently unfair for anyone to put another human being in this position. If the privilege is to be granted at all, it should be only to small children. It is a right they should lose automatically at age thirteen. Nonetheless, there are those who ask it. Vanity is generally the motive. It creates an entire body of discipline. You must resist the temptation to tell the truth.

Who among us hasn't had the urge, when asked by a middle-aged woman to guess her age, to respond by saying something like, "With or without makeup?"

How many times has an older man or woman asked, "How old do you think I am?" You want to respond by saying, "Old enough to have the world's worst breath, and more liver spots than a kid with measles."

When a fourteen-year-old boy poses the question, which is rare, you have to rein in the comment, "Not old enough to have grown into your nose yet."

And the teen princess wants to hear something flattering about her face or form. Don't ever say, "Obviously, you're quite a young lady, just not old enough to have tits."

As for the middle-aged man who challenges your honesty, it is difficult to resist the temptation to say, "You look pretty good, with the legs and face of a man half your age, and the belly of one twice as old."

Alas, we can't say what we want, even when we're asked to play the guessing game. And there is danger here. The danger is the possibility, and in some cases the probability, of guessing too high. You must always remember that the question is being asked because the person asking it does not believe he or she looks his or her age. They're proud of it. If you guess too high, in the case of all women and most men, or too low, in the case of most seniors, you have been coerced into an insult.

Insults are something we like to avoid on most occasions. Although there are ways of doing it without the person on the receiving end realizing it (see "How to Insult People in Ways That Make You Feel Good and That Make Them Believe Is a Compliment").

We can dispose of the senior first. Your response should be, "I don't know how old you are, but you look better than I do." It will be greeted with some disappointment, but better safe than sorry.

To the middle-aged man, try something like, "I don't know, but you still look like you could go ten rounds with Julia Roberts."

He'll like that. Come to think of it, the older guy might like it too.

Now for the woman who asks. Women never ask such a question until they are in their forties, fifties, or older. Younger women don't dare risk the chance of being told they look older than they are. The older women usually are desperate to be told they look younger—men too, for that matter, though they like that notion that no matter what their virility is unquestioned.

For starters, you can tell the woman that she looks like she could still go ten rounds with Brad Pitt. If she doesn't blush, answer forty. If she does, say twenty-nine.

As a matter of fact, forty is a pretty good age for most women who would ask the question. My experience tells me that the question is most often asked by women between the ages of forty-three and fifty-seven. So, forty will usually work very nicely.

There may be a time when a woman will ask you to guess her age, and using my formula, you guess twenty-nine. If she tells you she's really fifty, THEN tell her she looks like she could go ten rounds with you. After your answer, she probably will.

Chapter 23

To People Who Complain About Being Overweight

It must be genetically embedded in the fat cell. People who are overweight tend to complain about it publicly. I suspect it is a psychological attempt to elicit either sympathy or expressions of denial from those within earshot. Overweight people desperately want to hear that they are not as heavy as they are or look as bad as they feel they do. Truth of the matter is, they know very well what they look like. They know all too completely how difficult it is to find clothes that fit and look good, and how difficult it is to get into and out of a chair.

I sympathize. I could lose a few pounds myself. However, I know how I got this way. I eat too much. I simply have no patience with my heavy friends who bemoan some genetic accident or who suggest a glandular deficiency, then sit down to a meal heavy on starch and fat and wash it down with cake and ice cream.

I have many fat friends and value their friendship. However, the source of their problem is never a mystery to me once I sit down to dinner with them. Invariably, they choose the menu items that are richest in all the things that contribute to their weight problem. Just watch them check out at the supermarket. Their shopping basket often looks like an Oreo farm in the midst of a potato chip forest surrounded by lakes of sugar-laden sodas.

I have a friend who is seventy-five pounds overweight and wonders why. On a business trip, we went to a nice restaurant that specialized in fish. He ordered a Brandy Alexander, then a second. He was heavily into the rolls before he'd finished his second drink. He "appetized" on mozzarella cheese sticks. For his entree, he supped on a sixteen-ounce Steak Diane, a baked potato with cheddar cheese and sour cream, and a nice salad with Roquefort dressing. He topped it off with pecan pie smothered with ice cream and washed it all down with Irish Coffee. He truly is what he eats.

I know there are people out there with glandular problems, and that science is now suggesting that obesity can be inherited or is otherwise unavoidable. That is truly sad; however, science will undoubtedly learn how to deal with these errant genes and glands. As for the rest of us, we have to eat more intelligently and exercise more.

Nonetheless, it is a difficult position to be put in when an overweight person complains about being overweight. To begin with, obesity invites laughter. For whatever the reason, fat people make us laugh. We should not, but we do. It is not fat people who are jolly, as the legend suggests, it is the people around them. My first advice to heavy people is, don't talk about it. People will tend to snicker.

I would also suggest that they not make fun of themselves. If they do, folks will tend to go along with the gag. If you give people an opening and say, in effect, my size is fair game, they will play along.

It is also my suggestion that conversations with heavy people tend to be stilted. People try to avoid certain words, as they rightly should. Some of the words one should work very hard at avoiding are *fat, cream* (especially *heavy cream*), *donuts, exercise, porky, calories, specific gravity, gordo, lite, fat free, mayonnaise, Twinkie, pizza, chunky, peanut butter, deep fat, skinny, flat belly, whipped cream,* and *spare tire.* There are many, many more. However, these words have a triggering capacity and tend to make heavy people morose and even more inclined to talk about being overweight.

Words that tend to get people off the subject are *diet, carrots, bulemia, parsley, fish, salad, scale* (this can go the other way), *Slim-Fast, Jenny Craig, anorexia, lettuce, heart disease,* and *Weight Watchers.*

A discussion about weight is territory heavy people don't wish to explore, fearing it will cause their conversation partners to offer unsolicited advice. They are rarely happy to receive such advice. But sometimes a heavy friend is desperate for council and help but too afraid or embarrassed to ask for it outright. In some cases, they will ask for it in code. The aforementioned words can be a clue.

If your friend says:

"I'm thinking of buying a carrot farm . . ."

"I'm turning into a parsley freak . . ."

"I read where eating fish can give you a heart attack . . ."

"Did anyone ever die from throwing up?"

"Please put a leaf of lettuce on that pizza . . ."

Such talk can be considered a strong signal that your friend wants to do something about his or her weight. It is appropriate to offer some weight-loss advice and encouragement.

On the other hand, these comments are signals to mind your own business:

"Flat bellies piss me off."

"I dream of donuts with whipped cream on them, and I'm gonna get me some after this pizza."

"I killed a guy last night for calling me 'Porky.'"

"I'm going to put a dab of mayonnaise on that peanut butter."

"Are you finished with that fried chicken? Can I have it?"

"I understand calories are units of heat. I'm feeling a little chilly, so I guess I'll order a pizza."

"I would never get into my car without taking my spare tire. What are you laughing at, asshole?"

This person is not ready for a diet and is not reaching out for help. Avoid jokes about his or her size.

Above all else, don't call him "Porky."

And this final note: Be especially careful when the weight issue comes up with a spouse. My final advice should be evident except to the complete dullard.

When a woman enters the room in a new dress and asks, "Does this dress make me look fat?" Refrain from the temptation to answer honestly. The only answer is an emphatic "NO!"

I know of a marriage that was irretrievably broken when a woman in a new frock entered the room and asked her mate, "On a [here's that dangerous word] scale of one to ten, does this dress make me look fat?" His response cost him his marriage, "Why don't you waddle [another word to avoid] over to the scale and figure it out for yourself."

All he lost was his marriage. He should consider himself lucky he did not lose much more than that.

Chapter 24

On Lying

We are all liars. Yes, we are. We don't call it lying. We call it fibbing, or we claim to tell "little white lies." Most of us do it to protect someone else. Therefore, when that's the case, there is honor in it.

We would never tell a friend we think his or her baby is unattractive, even if we believe the child makes a monkey look like the Gerber Baby. If we don't want to go to a party, we don't say it. We make up an excuse. It's lying, but lying with a noble purpose. Sort of. Because that *lie* is a *fib*, a kinder gentler word. We fib on the phone. We fib at work. We fib all the time.

No one can abide the person who lies to deceive maliciously, to mislead for personal gain, or to harm another. But fibs, promoting innocent deception, which extricate us from an annoying situation, gain us no more than a little free time and the avoidance of boredom, and protect rather than harm, are, indeed, honorable. At least they are not mean-spirited.

Yes, fibs are among the most recognized and time-honored means of avoiding embarrassment, insult, or anything else we don't like.

This book is written in a humble attempt to preserve the fib as an art form, while not hurting anyone in the process.

Honest!